Meant to Be

Dale Macdonald

Cover Photo:

Dale and his life partner Eileen Connors enjoying a pleasant walk by the Salish Sea in Sechelt, B.C.

Contents

CHAPTER ONE 1

CHAPTER TWO 18

CHAPTER THREE 33

CHAPTER FOUR 48

CHAPTER FIVE 59

CHAPTER SIX 76

CHAPTER SEVEN 91

CHAPTER EIGHT 107

CHAPTER NINE 126

CHAPTER TEN 138

CHAPTER ELEVEN 150

CHAPTER TWELVE 165

CHAPTER THIRTEEN 180

CHAPTER FOURTEEN 196

CHAPTER FIFTEEN 209

CHAPTER SIXTEEN 230

CHAPTER SEVENTEEN 249

CHAPTER EIGHTEEN 267

CHAPTER NINETEEN 278

CHAPTER TWENTY 295

CHAPTER TWENTY-ONE 306

CHAPTER TWENTY-TWO 318

CHAPTER TWENTY-THREE 334

CHAPTER TWENTY-FOUR 350

CHAPTER TWENTY-FIVE 366

CHAPTER TWENTY-SIX 375

CHAPTER TWENTY-SEVEN 389

CHAPTER TWENTY-EIGHT 402

CHAPTER TWENTY-NINE 414

CHAPTER THIRTY 430

Chapter One

Moving day arrived, and the move had gone well. No items had been damaged, something of particular concern for Brad Webster. He had nice things and wanted to keep them that way, especially his antique, glass-fronted barrister bookcase. Overall, the movers had done a good job except for one man's light overspray in the downstairs bathroom. Brad tore off some toilet paper, wiped the rim of the toilet bowl and thought, *You'd think he'd know he sprinkled and give it a wipe himself. Damn! He even got some on the floor.*

As he watched the movers drive away, he was left with the implications of the choices he and his girlfriend Karen had made in Vancouver. The most obvious being that setting up in Sechelt would be a solo performance. *A hell of a way to start out,* he thought. *But it takes two to untie a Gordian knot, and if I changed my mind, I know she wouldn't change hers.*

He walked into the living room, where a chaos of boxes and ill-placed furniture quietly sat as if in judgment of him. Though not yet noon, he reached into a packing box for a bottle of tequila he thought to bring and poured a couple of ounces into a small glass, topping it with a bit of water. In the living room, he dropped into one of his leather recliners and gazed at the confusion surrounding him, a disarray reflecting his emotional state. He sipped his drink, allowing himself some quiet contemplation about the why of their breakup. Consternation lines began playing over his face as he began thinking about what had transpired, but nothing substantive came to light. The voltage was there, but the wiring was askew.

Brad's drawn-out journey to the Sunshine Coast began in Calgary, his hometown. As an only child, he had been raised in a way that people in the know say enhances a child's creativity, feeds independence and the ability to entertain oneself. He did grow up with his father's sense of accomplishment, something he routinely showed, whether on a playing field or in a classroom. In his teens, he showed an innate ability to write short stories, even if only for himself. Still, he wanted to learn how to write well-composed sentences and how to punctuate properly. Much of it he already knew. When he graduated from high school, his father gave him *The Elements of Style,* a book written by authors Strunk and White. It taught good composition, proper punctuation, sentence fluency, strong sentences, and omitting needless words – good writing.

Soon afterward, Brad enrolled in one of the University of Calgary's creative writing workshops. When he graduated, his father congratulated him, saying, "Son, you're on the track to endless possibilities." He happily added, "To begin, you can now live in your own space. My tenant is leaving, and you can move into the laneway."

Brad said, “I don’t have much income yet, and it’ll take some time.”

His father replied with a quote, as he often did, “Slow and steady wins the race.” He added, “Don’t worry about it. And what’s more, I want you to have a much-deserved holiday to learn something about the greater world.” Brad spent nearly two months visiting countries from the UK to Greece, gaining a much-expanded worldview as his father had anticipated.

At the beginning of the following month, he moved into the laneway, which had been his father’s pet rental home for the past two years. An attractive smaller space with one bedroom, a kitchen, a bathroom, a living room and a utility room. Brad would pay little rent, and with low expenses, he began freelance writing. Several months later, with the best examples of his writing, he approached Calgary’s StarMetro newspaper and was hired to write mainly local business features. One year later, he had developed restless feet. It was not about the job; it was about not being where he wanted to be. He had been in Vancouver years earlier with his parents, and he remembered the first time he stood onshore and gazed at the ocean's broad and inviting horizon that promised adventure. Since then, Vancouver has been where he wanted to be.

With restless feet and riding a tidal wave of anticipation, Brad quit the newspaper and drove to Vancouver. His first challenge would be to rent an apartment. He found an affordable semi-furnished place on Pendrell Street in Vancouver's West End. His father, ever thoughtful, sent some essential furniture items: a table and chairs and, more importantly, a new bed and mattress.

Within a month, at age twenty-three, he secured a job writing for Vancouver's Exelmor Business Magazine. During this period, he met his future wife, Linda, a tall and attractive young woman who also worked in the publishing industry. They were married a year later, and within three years, they had a son, Gavin, and a daughter, Marie. By the time eight years had passed, so had their marriage for irreconcilable differences. The primary problem was her preternatural jealousy that Brad said put them on completely separate tracks. It didn't matter where he went or what woman he might casually look at; she would make his life miserable with accusations and threats of breakup.

Brad was a good-looking man, but he wasn't a "player." Though a sad turn of events, the breakup happened. The bond with his children remained strong, and he usually spent time with them on Saturdays or Sundays. My favorite restaurant was always popular. A variety of hikes, including North Vancouver's mountainside Grouse Grind, were often part of their outdoor agenda.

Exelmor did little to inspire Brad. After a five-year hitch, he accepted an offer of employment with a similar publication that promised more of everything. Four years later, it hadn't matched his expectations, and he began to have thoughts about starting his own magazine. Months later, with money from his ethical investment fund and encouraged by the experience gained at the previous two magazines, Brad put together Coast Leisure Magazine, focusing on Vancouver's good life. He hired two employees: secretary Daphne Leigh and salesman Dave Elrick, both from the publishing industry. Brad's well-focused goals saw the magazine flourish, garnering ever more advertisers with yet more stories, most of them written by him.

He didn't spend all of his time at the office. *God forbid!* He especially enjoyed his business and leisure trips from Vancouver to Lund at the north end. He never failed to be impressed with the Sunshine Coast's calm and natural beauty. In his mind, Vancouver's hustle and bustle had lost its shine, and the town of Sechelt, located between Gibsons and Lund, best illustrated the benefits of coastal life.

Moreover, it was only a forty-minute ferry ride from Vancouver. Brad had always wanted to retire at age fifty, and doing it in Sechelt became his ultimate goal.

By the time he turns forty-six, he is certain about how and when he'll move to Sechelt. In the meantime, he stays unmarried. His problem is that he likes younger women who eventually want to get married. But he doesn't, at least not yet. He soon meets thirty-five-year-old Karen Lacey, he then being forty-six. She was with a media girlfriend at a function introducing some of CBC's upcoming television programming. Advertising agencies and publications attend and find such events helpful in planning their client's overall media advertising. She is a successful notary public, stylish, attractive and very uptown in her social world. That night, she looked absolutely haut monde. They were both single and unattached and two weeks later began dating.

When Brad took Karen with him to another media event, he found they weren't entirely in step.

The event included a small orchestra for dance time after program presentations had been concluded. While they comfortably sat at a small table, the music began.

Brad stood up. “Come on, honey, let’s dance,” and so saying, he took her by the hand and led her to the dance floor as she lightly resisted. As he held her close, she stammered, “I have to tell you I’m not much of a dancer of regular dance steps. I’d like to do it my way. You do it your way.”

She proceeded to make some impressive pot-dancing moves with some shimmy movements. His moves were much less dynamic – routine.

Back at their table, he looked at her inquiringly. “Have you ever learned to dance regular dance steps … like the two-step?”

She shook her head. “Most of us didn’t. We thought it looked in some ways old fashioned.”

He looked at her intently with a smile on his

face, thinking, *I'll have you dancing. You'll see.*

He also discovered that they were also moderately out of step in their vital and separate personal worlds. It isn't surprising that they lived apart, choosing not to restrict their independence and zeal for their work and time demands. While their workloads might've been similar, their romance couldn't be as clearly defined. Their relationship had respect, good communication, affection and passion, but some less definable aspects were missing. Their differing social mores were obvious: she enjoyed the camaraderie of business associates, but by the end of the day, he had had enough of business interactions and the people involved.

Her heavily socialized business life often kept her away. He trusted her and accepted her need to participate with the business people and functions within her industry. Her preternatural need to connect with industry associates presented one evening when they were out for dinner. She noticed two male business acquaintances sitting at a table on the other side of the restaurant waving at her. She turned to him, “Should we invite them to join us?” Before she could say another word, he responded, saying, “If I saw a couple of women I know, would you like it if I asked them to join us?” She thought about it for a moment, and nothing more was said. To him, her capricious suggestion was like a slap, and it put a damper on the entire evening. At home that night, he couldn’t help feeling that she liked to spend too much of her time with her associates, most of them men. And because she often said little about her evenings away from him, he couldn’t help wondering about who she might be spending time with. He often had the urge to phone her late at night or do a drive-by, but he never did. Best to leave it alone.

Days later, during an evening together at Brad’s place, Karen’s business associations again wended into their conversation. After dinner, as they sat on the sofa having green tea, she placed her hand on his knee. “Don’t forget the society dinner party on Saturday night. You *are* coming with me, aren’t you?”

He looked at her and nodded slowly. “I said I'd go to the more formal occasions with you, but not your little get-togethers with the other notaries.”

“They’re called information sessions, and we go for dinner afterward, and you’re always welcome to attend for dinner. I’d like that.”

He thought for a moment. “I think it’s important that you go and enjoy yourself with your associates. It’s your business world, just like I have mine. Besides, I like *our* dinners out, with just you and me. And if we can dance, so much the better.”

“She looked at him, amused, and said, “You and your dancing… like you’re another Arthur Murray.”

He laughed and reached for her hand. “Come on. I’ll hum a tune, and you can follow along with me.”

Taking her into his arms, he began humming *Dance Me to the End of Love*.

She winced and kissed him, "Sorry, but I don't get the rhythm."

He smiled and said, "A bit of practice will do wonders … and speaking of practice, the evening's still young." He gestured toward the bedroom.

Karen nodded but didn't stay the night. She had an early morning meeting.

Their relationship had slowed Brad's thoughts about retiring, but by the time three years had passed, their frolicsome relationship began to show cracks. It was a case of a young woman with an older man and the challenges it can present. Karen wanted to get married and have children; her mother wanted grandchildren, putting yet more pressure on her. Add to this her age, thirty-eight, so often a fuse point in a woman's perception of her declining childbearing years. Even though Brad said he didn't want to start another family at his age, Karen had been hopeful that their love would eventually soften his stance. But he complicated the matter by looking at the concept from an oblique angle, making it conveniently recessive. As weeks and months flew by, the issue would drift in and out of focus, making marriage and children like neverland. Earlier in their relationship, Brad thought they were on the same track, but as time went on, he realized that they remained in separate worlds.

To make their relationship yet more challenging, ever since his divorce, he felt that a loving couple needn't be married to enjoy living together. It may or may not be true, but what is true is that unsolved relationship issues don't simply disappear. Rather than meet the issue head-on, both of them continued to merely pick at it. She had for some time thought about the kinds of things to say to allay his fears. "I read about a couple the other day who had a unique solution to their similar impasse." She looked at him to make certain he was listening.

“Tell me about it,” he said skeptically.

“They thought they'd get married, and if children were born, they'd buy a duplex, and he'd live on one side and she on the other side with the children. And that way, there could be a family environment or breaks from it when needed.”

He couldn’t help but chuckle. “You made that up. It sounds like a plan made by a mad hatter.”

The conversation ended with her wondering what was a mad hatter. Brad mightn’t talk much about his wish for retirement, but it was always on his mind. He could start a new beginning with money in the bank, good growth stocks and buying a home with no mortgage.

It finally reached the point of thinking more about it on a Tuesday morning as he listened to an angry advertiser’s unwarranted phone complaint about a missed full-page ad placement. When he told the man the ad order had been received too late for the current issue, it turned into a big argument. It wasn't the first time the man was late. When Brad hung up, stressed – fed up, actually – he realized he was ready to step away from the big-city pace of life. He had viable options as to when to do it. He'd have adequate financial backing, selling his house and business. Two years earlier, he had sold his parent's house and Lane's home. They had both died of cancer six months apart. He was an only child and the beneficiary of the buildings.

The balance of their estate went primarily to family relatives. He was in a fortunate financial position that would provide more than ample funds for buying a house in Sechelt. They normally cost about half as much or less as a similar place in Vancouver. Then there was his company. In the meantime, he had to think about his employees, Daphne and Dave. He'd give them both high recommendations and generous separation pay, but he'd feel badly letting them go. They were friends, and he'd miss them.

For Brad and Karen, a happy future together depended on a solution that would be favorable for both of them. His plan was straightforward: he'd sell his business and his Kitsilano house, buy a house in Sechelt and move there. Unfortunately, her options weren't as clear. She was a successful Vancouver notary public and owned a condo. And what about doing her work – how would she, could she? Her continuum was as clear as mud, leaving her in total limbo.

Chapter Two

At Brad's house one wintery Saturday evening a few weeks before Christmas, their dogged dilemma again knocked on the door. They were in the kitchen, where Karen stood with a glass of wine in her hand as Brad put a pot of water on a large burner. She stepped close to him. "We keep talking about it, but do you still think marriage isn't necessary for a couple to happily live together?"

He turned to her. "Believe it or not, it has become a social phenomenon in some countries. In Iceland, for example, more and more people are opting out of the need for marriage. In fact, I read that more than half the babies born there have parents who aren't married. The concept has caught on here, too, and an ever larger percentage of people are living together without marriage or are living alone."

"Is that what you want, to simply live in your place alone?"

“I don’t mean——“

“And what if I want children?”

“Karen, I can’t get my head around being a new father at my age. You know I’m going to be forty-nine in another month.”

“And I’m going on thirty-seven… not getting any younger,” she said, exasperated. “We’ve never seriously talked about it at any length, and I think it’s time to get some sense of direction. I’m not saying we have to come up with a master plan tonight. With time and business demands, we’ve both been too busy to sit down and seriously talk about it at any length. It’s like we’re afraid to discuss it, like being afraid to open the door of a spooky house for what we might discover inside. In the backs of our minds, we probably believe we have a workable plan, but we don’t, and it’s increasingly on my mind.”

He put his arm around her. “We just have to take some quiet time to work things out.” He looked at the window and pointed at the rivulets of water streaming down. “This constant rain is getting to me. I've been meaning to ask you how you feel about going to Mexico again for a two-week holiday and talking more about our future without distraction. Do it like we did last year and go to Merida at the start of the second or third week in January. I can do it if you can. It’ll be my treat.”

She stepped back and set her wine glass on the counter. “I don’t know, Brad. I’m getting pretty busy right now. My new client wants me to meet with him to discuss ongoing aspects of his new development.”

“We could go at a less busy point in your business. We can both work it out.”

She moved in front of him, kissed him and said, “And it’s also your birthday at the end of January. So leave it with me. I’ll see what I can do.”

At that moment, a swirling piece of music could be heard on the living room stereo. He grabbed her hand. “Come on, let’s dance.”

She hesitated. “You conveniently forget I can’t dance to music like that.”

“Come on, it’s a simple two-step.”

They began with him leading, and she tried to follow or anticipate the next move, but her efforts were hesitating and slow. He had been a dancer ever since his mother taught him when he was a teenager. He had always wished that he and Karen could dance and experience the synchronized togetherness and pleasure it can provide. But it had been near impossible to influence her to get in step. She’d rather dance her way.

Christmas soon arrived, and they spent it at Brad’s house. This year, his daughter Marie was able to be there. She was studying to become a dentist. Karen had no siblings, and her parents lived in London, Ontario, a distance traveled but once a year or less. It was always a toss-up as to who would do the traveling. They'd have come this Christmas if her mother had more fully recovered from a knee replacement. That evening, as they talked excitedly about their upcoming trip to Merida, Marie innocently said, “So what do you think you two will be up to this time next year? Any marriage plans?”

Brad looked at Karen. “Funny you should ask. We’ve talked about it, but we haven’t figured out things like time frame or logistics.”

“You mean like moving and stuff like that?” Gavin intoned. “And which place to live in?”

Brad thought for a moment and nodded. “Well, something like that.”

Marie picked up on their reluctance to discuss it. “I went to Cancun a couple of years ago and planned to go to Merida but never made it. I hear It's a very nice city. I wish I could be there with you.”

The conversation had been artfully turned around, and discussions about Mexico, pyramids, and individual travel experiences prevailed during dinner and the rest of the evening.

On the third weekend in January, the couple checked into Merida's Gran Hotel just as they had done the previous year when they celebrated Brad's forty-eighth birthday. Again, they enjoyed the hotel's Old World charm in Merida, the wrought iron trimmings, and the two interior floors with pillared balconies. The hotel's location was ideal, being within easy walking distance to the city center – the Zocalo.

They rented cars as needed and, on most days, visited Yucatan sites from pyramids to deep, water-filled limestone cenotes that looked like high-banked swimming pools. Traveling about and sight-seeing gave them the pleasure of interacting with local people and speaking Spanish. Brad had studied it at university, and Karen had taken private lessons.

On many mornings, they went to a coffee shop across the street to buy what was exceptionally flavorful Mexican coffee. They took their cups to a bench near the hotel and enjoyed the feel of a sunny winter morning in Mexico. As the sun rose higher and its warmth scattered the nighttime coolness, the air became pervaded with the scents of vegetation and cooking. Unlike the busy Zocalo, the area was calm, with mostly foot traffic. It was a place where friendly words were said to the couple, such as buen dia (good day) and hola (hello). Perhaps Brad's Canadian maple-leaf crest he routinely wore on his shirt had something to do with it.

A bit later in the morning, they'd walk to Abuela's restaurant at the Zocalo, their favorite restaurant, as on their previous visit. They liked the food and comfortable decor. For breakfast, actually brunch, Karen especially enjoyed the huevos rancheros, typically consisting of tortillas, eggs, tomato-chile sauce, refried beans, rice, avocado or guacamole. Brad liked that, too, but also their beef tamales and enchiladas. His favorite was chicken with mole poblano, which is a thick, rich red or brown sauce made with chilies, fruit, nuts, seeds and some chocolate, all as deliciously decadent as it sounds.

In the evening, they went again to Abuela's for their favorite selections. Then, in the cool of the evening, they sat at an outside table enjoying an after-dinner drink while observing the evening parade of tourists and locals. That night, it included a small boy and an even smaller girl who approached their table; they appeared to be around ages five and six.

The boy was selling Chiclets. When he said "Chiclets," he held out his tiny hand that held several small boxes, each containing two pieces of gum. Behind him stood the little girl carrying a cardboard tray of his ready supply.

Both children were well-dressed; they appeared to be clean and healthy. They weren't beggars. Brad had always been sympathetic and generous with children like these who were simply helping with family finances.

Karen slowly shook her head. "It's a shame to

see such young children having to do this."

Brad said, "I won't let him go without at least giving him some money."

He had a short conversation with the children and asked their names: he was Tomás, she was his sister, Maria.

When they left, Karen said, "They're so cute. I hope we'll see them again."

Brad nodded and said, "I'm sure we can count on it."

Before the children left, he took one box of gum, giving him and Karen one chiclet each. He paid generously, as always.

The next evening, as they again sat outside enjoying their after-dinner drink, Karen suddenly raised her glass. "Happy forty-ninth, sweetheart."

"Thank you my love. The twenty-third of the month *already*. I'd almost forgotten."

She smiled as she reached into her bag and

withdrew his birthday present, a replica of a Mayan in a full warrior's dress. "This guy kind of reminded me of you, ready for a hard day's fight."

He laughed at the comparison and the look of determination on the tiny man's face. "He'll be an inspiration when I need a pick-me-up."

"Like the scorpion, you gave me last year for my birthday."

"Yes, October's Scorpio figurine was made by one of Mexico's best sculptors. Solid cast bronze, with all parts absolutely authentic in detail.

The claws and tail stinger give inspiration toward achievement – nothing can get in the way." He looked at her. "And nothing really has, has it?"

She hesitated, "No, darling … nothing has."

Brad nodded encouragingly and said, "So, where did you get it?"

"When you went to get us coffee yesterday, I went to the shop next door. I liked the replica the first time I saw it."

Brad held it up and fixedly looked at it again. "I really like his costume and ready stance. Thanks again darling."

Tomás and Maria soon appeared as before, this time coming to the table with an air of familiarity and expectation. Brad and Karen were novel to the children because they not only spoke their language and were friendly but also communicated in an easy and non-deferential way. Tomás and Maria were seen as what they were: two children doing a helpful task entrusted to them by their parents.

Brad bent down to Tomás, asked about his father, and was told his father was sick.

Karen asked Maria about her mother and then turned to Brad. "I've forgotten what lavanderia means."

"She said her mother does laundry… for other people."

Karen slowly shook her head. “It’s almost unimaginable to see two tiny children like them sent out into the night to help raise money for the family.”

As young as they were, they understood the need. But did they see a mother’s angst at letting them go into the night? The children would, of course, be given instructions for their safety. Also important, they had the protection of being involved in and watched over by the Zocalo community. That night, Brad gave the children money, saying he’d buy Chiclets another time.

Tomás and Maria never failed to find the couple. Maria often pointed the way, she being Tomás’ able assistant. Maria particularly enjoyed Karen’s attention, whether she fussed with Maria’s hair or wiped a smudge. Brad and Karen always looked forward to seeing them, and within a few days, they were like their neighborhood children. The thing not known was the whereabouts of their home. Tomás seemed quite demure about it – at the instruction of his parents? – and he waved his hand in the general direction as if to say, "We live over there."

Thanks in part to their association with Tomás and Maria, the couple had enjoyed their holiday in a special way. Sadly, as is so often the case while on holidays, time flew by as if the wind had blown. On their last evening, they sat at their table feeling saddened that it'd be their final opportunity to enjoy their interaction with the children who'd become endeared to them. When the children saw them at their table, they approached with smiles on their faces. They were as happy seeing the couple as *they* were seeing the children.

Brad bought several boxes of Chiclets and, this time, gave Tomás a wad of Mexican money, telling him to put it in his pocket for his mother. Karen fussed with Maria; Brad made small talk with Tomás, who was ever the little man, business-like, polite and far too serious for a child his age, but understandable given the responsibility he shouldered.

The children looked perplexed when Brad told them this night would be the last time he and Karen would see them because they were returning home in the morning. When they told the children they were going back to their hotel, Tomás asked if they'd be here tomorrow. “No,” said Brad. And, making it clear to them, added, “Nuestra casa está en Canadá.” (Our home is in Canada) Tomás looked at Brad questioningly, “No aqui?” (not here?) Maria simply said, "Si?” Brad nodded. Karen crouched down and tearfully hugged Maria and Tomás; Brad shook Tomás’ hand.

Tomás looked from one of them to the other, thought about it for a moment and, because they had business to attend to, tugged on the cardboard tray for Maria to follow him. Then they walked away, two small children going alone into the night. Reaching the other side of the street, they suddenly turned and stood looking back. The moment was too much for

Karen, who let out a sob, accompanied by a deep sigh from Brad. Walking back to the hotel, they couldn't help feeling they were abandoning friends in need. They talked about things they might've done, should've done. But without knowing the parents' acceptance of them, it could be inappropriate, even pushy, to go further into their lives. They agreed they'd try to return next year to see the children and find out what they could do for their welfare and immediate needs.

That night in bed, Karen tearfully said she felt sorry for the children and wished there was time to do more. Brad surmised her motherly feelings were showing. She perhaps saw traits in Chapter 6 of Maria that she would hope to see in her own little girl someday. For the time being, at least, they'd leave the subject alone. There was so much more to discuss.

Chapter Three

As is often the case in troubled relationships, gremlins can pop up anytime and stir matters into frothy mind-twisters. It happened one evening when Karen was at Brad's house, sharing a pizza for dinner. He felt he could no longer ignore the increasing pressure of their impasse.

"Karen, we need to talk more about my plan to retire. I'm going to do it, but it could get complicated. You have to help me so we can be on track together. As you know, I presented an offer to sell my business to Exelmor. We've retained a good relationship, and they're interested. I'm sure it will happen. My magazine's theme and readership are a good add-on for them. So here's my plan: I'll sell the magazine, then the house and look for another one in Sechelt. And, honey, you're a part of the plan. So please check out your options so we can work out what's best for you."

She put down her knife and fork and looked at

him pointedly. “I suppose I could commute to Vancouver for some of it … or open a Sechelt office. But it wouldn’t be easy. And am I to go there as your girlfriend or as your wife? What a question to have to ask, and (she teared up) it makes me very unhappy.”

He reached for her hand. “Sweetheart, these are all things we, of course, have to discuss. As far as the move is concerned, there are many reasons why I have to get on with it. I need to put things together for a meeting with Exelmor next week. Something else to consider is the expected recession that will have an immediate effect on real estate. People will begin selling homes, and as fast as they sell, prices will drop. We’d both have to sell soon and not have our freedom of movement curtailed by a protracted financial slump that will affect both of our properties. If the bottom drops out of the real estate market, it could mean being stuck in place for years. It’s something we’ll both have to think about. In the meantime, we’ll have to seriously work things out.”

Karen grimaced. “I understand that. But I still don’t want to move to Sechelt unless we get married.”

“I do know that, but the having children part of it is something I can’t get my head around … the concept of raising them for twenty years until I’m almost seventy.” She stared at him, lost for words.

Exelmor bought Brad’s business in late March; he soon after listed his house for sale. Being in Kitsilano on Vancouver’s popular West Side would be a key selling advantage. Within two weeks, the house sold for more than the listed price. This and the sale of his business added to financial security that would make for happy house hunting in Sechelt. He was fortunate that his Vancouver friend Jeffrey Bacstrom, a radio sales representative, could recommend a Sunshine Coast ace realtor named Fred Vallevand.

“He always has a solid client base and is a top seller,” Jeffrey said. “Let him know in advance what you're looking for, and he'll sniff it out for you. He won't waste your time."

Brad contacted Vallevand and arranged for a date to look at suitable Sechelt homes.

Meanwhile, Karen was going through a personal hell trying to think logically about what to do. A call to her mother solved nothing; it only made things worse.

"Well, Karen, you know how I feel. The concept of going along with no mutual goal usually ends up on a dead-end street. You'd like to have children just as much as I'd like to have grandchildren."

"But, Mom, Brad thinks he's too old to start a family."

"Well, maybe he is. Face it, sweetie, in this kind of circumstance, I think you really do have to consider the possibility of ending it and getting on with your life."

The conversation ended with them both

agreeing that perhaps Brad's imminent change in circumstances might change his mind – at least regarding marriage.

Unfortunately, the only thing that changed on Brad's mind was a pumped-up urgency to buy a Sechelt house as soon as possible. He couldn't wait to be able to enjoy it in the Sunshine Coast's ultra-natural surroundings. His previous times spent there, of course, included business trips. But it was a long-weekend camping trip with a couple of friends that showed it best. Their travels took them from the Langdale ferry, near Gibsons, to Lund at the north end of the coastal highway. Nearby Egmont is the home of the famous Skookumchuck Narrows, having what is said to be the largest saltwater rapid in North America, and the second fastest one in the world. Brad and his friends enjoyed seeing its fury, but next time they'd try to be there during a high tide and experience an even more dynamic show. They also enjoyed the natural environment, all of it a refreshing contrast to big-city life.

With a population of around twelve hundred, Sechelt has one of the highest seniors populations in the province, with a median age in the mid-to-late fifties. Other communities up and down the coast had similar demographics. Brad thought about how the women he'd meet might often be older, at least older than those in his experience. But becoming part of the fabric of the community and being a productive part of it would be his biggest concern.

At the same time, he'd make new friends with whom to participate in activities such as hiking and volunteering, and other things like dining out and dancing. His vibe would attract his tribe. He'd meet people with similar interests, such as he enjoyed with his longtime friend Jeffrey. As someone always under pressure selling radio-advertising time in Vancouver, he understood the kind of atmosphere needed in which to simply relax and distress. So he was a good person to share time with, a good conversationalist, with intelligence and a quick wit. He and Brad always enjoyed a drink together at a favorite pub, and did it without a constant rehashing of sports scores, business triumphs, and relationship problems.

They could, of course, discuss such things and also get a bit raunchy now and then, such as when Jeffrey once suggested they go to Vegas for the long weekend, take in some shows, and meet some girls. Not a good idea, Brad thought, for multiple reasons – his relationship with Karen for one. Jeffrey, on the other hand, had recently broken up with a girlfriend and simply sought mollifying. Boys will be boys, but their reason to meet for a night out was usually an unexpressed need to relax with a friend, without long and boring pronouncements of any kind. Better to have some meaningful conversation and a few laughs with which to enjoy drinks and dinner.

Typical was their evening together before Brad moved to Sechelt. As he often did, Jeffrey brought to the conversation yet another intriguing media newsroom story that the general public often didn't hear about.

He took a sip of beer and said, "Did you hear about the dead man found in a recycling bin yesterday?" Brad shook his head.

"The guy driving the garbage truck was about to dump one of those blue bins into the truck when he discovered a man's body inside. Police said it had been suicide. It's kind of like a Shakespearean story of love and betrayal. The man had lost his job through layoffs and, as if that wasn't bad enough, he discovered his wife and a neighbor were having a red-hot relationship. Confrontation apparently did nothing to settle matters. The man began to drink himself silly, ergo his demise."

"Did he shoot himself?"

"No, nothing as messy as that. He got into the bin and apparently ingested something. No word yet about what it could have been."

“Wow, that’s some story.”

Jeffrey had a sip of beer. “And there’s more. He left a note for his wife. He said if he continued to live, there are terrible things he might do. So he decided to do the lesser of two evils.”

Brad shook his head. “The martyr syndrome, you could say.”

“I guess so.”

“Interesting tale. He could have sold the house, taken his share and started over.”

Jeffrey nodded. “But you have to understand the man’s turmoil.”

“It'd be a tough situation all round, but it didn’t have to be the end. It could be a new beginning. And speaking of new beginnings, I’m selling my magazine to Exelmor.”

“I didn’t know you were that far into negotiations.”

“It’s an easy add-on for them. When the sale’s

completed I'm going to put my house up for sale and look for a house in Sechelt. It's taken quite a while for me to get to this point."

"Then what will you do?"

"Once I'm settled, I'll begin to plan the next chapter."

"Is Karen part of the plan?"

Brad put down his glass and thought for a moment. "It's something we're working on. As you know, we have different thoughts about starting a family. I don't want to be a new father at my age. I used to think we were on the same page, but this could be the end of the line. We're at a difficult point where we'll each have to make some honest choices for our future."

Jeffrey nodded appraisingly. "Well, we all have to make relationship decisions in our lives, some tougher than others."

Brad put up his hand. "I remember you telling

me about the beautiful radio sales girl you once dated and had to quit because she drank too much and got–"

Jeffrey said, "Something I'd rather forget. By the way, and I know it's not your favorite subject to talk about, but did you know that, after serving only two years, Leonard Mason is scheduled for early release?"

Brad looked shocked. "I didn't think he'd be out for at least another year."

"Well, it is a surprise, but remember he got charged with manslaughter. I looked it up and it can mean homicide committed without intent, but with reckless disregard for another's life. In any case, he's getting statutory release after serving two-thirds of his sentence. It sounds weird, but he can serve the last third of his sentence in the community. It means he has to be good, abide by laws and parole rules."

Brad shook his head. "I never heard the details before, and I don't care now. I'd rather forget him."

“It can be a case of good behavior and a lockup being too crowded that allows this to happen.” He paused, had a sip of beer, and put his glass on the table. “I've meant to ask you why you didn’t simply refuse to testify.”

“Well, it’s not as easy as that. I foolishly hung around until the police arrived. I wanted to see Mason get arrested and hauled away. Big mistake. They more or less corralled us and asked who saw the fight. One guy near me put up his hand, and then pointed at me and said, 'He did, too.'”

“I couldn’t lie at that point. Then when the court contacted me and I said I’d rather not testify. I soon discovered that if you do go to court and refuse to answer questions that the judge allows, you can be found in contempt of court and maybe even jailed for a short time.”

Jeffrey shook his head. “Wow. That sounds pretty severe. You could probably get a lawyer to help your case.”

“But what if he got a lawyer to fight my testimony? Nothing about his actions would surprise me. He was always a pain in the ass.”

“Sounds like you can’t trust him to be rational. You might want to keep an eye out for him.”

Brad looked at Jeffrey inquiringly, “What do you mean?”

“You remember him pointing his manacled hands at you as he was being taken from the courtroom and sent to prison? There might've been a message in it.”

“I knew him to be antagonistic and vengeful. But now with a prison record, I’m sure he’ll rethink things and be somewhat rehabilitated.”

Jeffrey smiled, “We can only hope.”

Brad put down his empty glass. “I doubt he’ll be some kind of mad-dog ex-con. But I'll pay attention to what I hear about him. And you can tell me if you hear of anything I should know.”

“Will do, amigo.”

The Leonard Mason fiasco had happened two years previously as Brad and Jeffrey were approaching their favorite pub on Robson Street. Two men could be seen in a heated argument near the entrance. It soon progressed to trading punches. One man’s punch quickly dropped the other to his knees, but he came up swearing and relaunching his attack. Before he completely got to his feet, he received a vicious kick to the throat. He dropped like a stone, thrashed for a moment, and became still. Brad recognized his assailant as Leonard Mason from high school days in Calgary. He had the same large nose and malicious eyes.

Mason had been a pugnacious bully, always looking for a fight. Police and ambulance quickly attended. Witnesses were asked to provide their evidential information. The coroner’s report later determined death was caused by a severely torn carotid artery. When Brad was in the witness stand,

Mason glowered at him. And while being led from the courtroom he, as Jeffrey said, accusingly pointed his manacled hands at Brad. Mason had always shown himself to be a nasty and vengeful piece of work. Now, with his scheduled release, Brad would keep tabs on him to know his whereabouts, and not be caught unaware.

Chapter Four

In her relationship problem with Brad, Karen had kept herself together—sane, she called it—by spending some time with close friends. Typical was her best friend, Allison, who'd invited her for dinner rather than going to a restaurant. She knew some highly emotional things Karen might want to discuss would be better aired at home. Dinner was planned for Sunday evening, with drinks at five.

Karen arrived early, looking anxious and troubled. "Hi, Allison. I know there's only one thing worse than someone coming late, and that's someone coming too early. But I was feeling restless."

Being good friends, they laughed and hugged before Allison's happy response, "Being early is a lot better than not being here at all." They had known each other since high school and enjoyed the kind of repartee usual in long friendships. Allison poured two glasses of wine, and they relaxed on her sofa. An impressive view of Vancouver's North Shore mountains spread before them, one of the advantages of living in the West End on the twenty-first floor.

"Well, here's to friendship and the other good things in life," Allison said, raising her glass.

"To friendship," Karen murmured. "I wish I could say to the rest, too." She put down her glass and looked at Allison searchingly. "Have you ever been in love and began to think it might be with the wrong man?"

Allison nodded enthusiastically. "Hell yes." "But how much time were you prepared to give it before doing something about it?"

"It depends on whether or not there is any chance of things being turned around—either that or end it." Karen stared at her glass. "That's where I am with Brad. We can't find a solution that's agreeable to both of us…the having children part."

Allison knew the entire story and had told her on a previous occasion that the problem would probably be insurmountable. But now she'd hear Karen out and try in some way to be helpful. “The thing is that neither of you has said straight out that it’s either this way or the highway. You've become too used to the situation and stay on the fringes; nothing constructive happens one way or the other. And you both have such opposing viewpoints there seems to be no happy solution. You’re stalled in the headwinds of a dilemma.” She snickered. “I read that somewhere.”

Karen began to tear up. “We’ve tried to cross to each other’s side of things, but now it’s like the bridge has been washed away.” Allison put her hand on Karen’s arm. “Okay, let’s be fair. Let’s look at it from Brad’s point of view, taking into account his age and so on.”

As they looked at it from his supposed viewpoint, they went this way and that, only ending up where they began. "Well, so much for psychological profiling and meaningful solutions," Allison said as she refilled their wine glasses. "Let's see if we can do any better in the kitchen." She invited Karen to join her while she began cooking steaks. Allison giggled. "I don't do this often, only when I'm having company. It's a nice changeup."

As they stood in the kitchen, they got caught up in their day-to-day activities as well as those of some of their friends and acquaintances.

Allison laughingly told about Dianne and Jimmy who planned to get married but changed their minds when they factored in the realization that there is more to it than just sex.

Meagan nodded in agreement, "Much more. Other important things like true love and affection … and children."

Allison looked at her, not sure what to say. She had some feelings about the matter that might be better left unsaid. For instance, children. She was

Karen's age and had no real desire to be a mother.

The steaks were soon cooked, the salad sat on the table, more wine had been poured, and the two friends were soon enjoying a delicious dinner, with, as Allison said, the added enjoyment of each other's company. By the end of the evening, little had been accomplished regarding Karen's plight.

Even so, their time together had been enjoyable and well spent, as usual.

Upon arriving at home, Karen felt the evening at Allison's place had been less comforting than usual. It being late, she fell on her bed and had a good cry. Nevertheless, before falling asleep, she felt she had gained greater insight into her problem that would help her deal with it in a more constructive and rational way. With hope in her heart and yet more questions in her mind, she eventually fell into a world of conflicting dreams.

It all came to a head at Brad's house on an evening they had planned to go out for dinner. He felt in a good mood, albeit somewhat circumspect. When he talked to Karen earlier in the day, the tone of her voice told him that something had changed. He knew she had recently had dinner at Allison's place and would have discussed their stalled relationship. And who knows what suggestions Allison might have made? He had every reason to think this night might be a pivotal point. Their overshadowing tensions had been exponentially developing since he sold his company. When the doorbell rang, he felt trepidation, like expecting a bill collector. He took a deep breath and opened the door.

Karen walked in looking stunning in black slacks and a floral-patterned gray blouse. She appeared to be in an unusually somber mood, not at all like her usual snappy businesswoman persona.

"Hi honey," Brad embraced her. "You look terrific."

"So do you."

She looked at him with only the trace of a smile.

He knew the time had come to once again open the discussion that had been too long covered by a cloud of obfuscation and upset. He went to the kitchen, poured each of them a glass of Merlot wine, and led her to the sofa.

He looked at her with concern. "So what's happening? Why so glum?"

She glanced away. "The time has come," the Walrus said..." She hesitated and gazed at him.

He nodded, knowingly. "To talk of many things, and I can see you have things you want to talk about."

"And I don't want to pretend I don't. We love each other, but love needs to be supported with mutual purpose. We're not on the same track, Brad. It's as if one of us has been derailed. And it's not me."

"Well, that depends on how you look at it. You've known from the beginning I don't want to start a family at my age, especially in retirement. Maybe I wasn't clear enough about it. And when I did attempt to make my point about it, you seemed to believe circumstances might change."

She looked at him piercingly, picked up her wine glass, and set it down again. "So where does it leave us now? You've sold the business and put your house up for sale, and all you have to do now is leave."

He had never heard her so upset, and he didn't want to make things worse. "Karen, it isn't like that at all," he said. "I love you and want you to be with me. You're the one who's making it difficult to move on."

She shook her head. "You don't give a damn about me. You have your life and a plan of how you want to live it … obviously without me."

"Karen, you're not listening to me. Your plan doesn't fit my concept of me in retirement. I need some time to think this through."

"How much more time?" she said, her eyes tearing.

He sat back and stared at his hands. “Maybe we have to be apart for a while and give ourselves some time and space to seriously evaluate our feelings, what we definitely want or don’t want.”

She couldn’t think of anything constructive to say. “I know it’s often done, but I never thought you and I'd come to this point, and it’s so damned sad.”

He kissed her now tear-stained face and held her as though frozen in the moment, unsure of what more could be said.

When she excused herself and went to the bathroom, he sat in a funk, having nothing encouraging or even affectionate to say to her. Considering the honest words that had been spoken, it'd be disingenuous to now launch into light banter or amorous inflections.

She returned, sat beside him, and looked at him intently.

Before she could say anything, he said, “As you

know, trial separations are often done to sort things out. How do you feel about us starting a one-month trial separation to sort things out?"

"But what if we wish to talk or get back together sooner? What if——"

"It only works if there's no contact for a month," he said softly.

"But like I said, what if one of us changes our mind sooner?"

"Karen, in that case, we should, of course, say so. Otherwise, we'll need the time to truly think it through. I'm concerned and stressed about maybe making the wrong decision in the matter, and in one way or another how it will affect my future and yours."

She sniffled. "So I just sit and wait."

"No, you don't just sit and wait. It's time for you too, to decide if you can change your mind," he explained. "It'll take both of us to determine the outcome. So we'll just have to wait and see. Let's be patient."

The evening concluded with them agreeing to a one-month trial separation with no contact. There being nothing more to discuss, dinner was canceled. At the door, they gazed into each other's eyes, both feeling the sting of potential loss as they held each other.

"I love you," she sadly murmured, with tears welling up again.

He looked at her with feeling. "I love you, too, darling."

After cheek kisses, she left, leaving him overwhelmed by sadness. He picked up his glass of wine, took a sip, and sat, reflecting on his feelings and the reasons behind them.

He sincerely hoped a month without contact would sort things out. But, as so often happens, the month passed with no contact, leaving only the detritus of a once-loving relationship–a fait accompli.

Chapter Five

On a sunny coastal day in April, Brad stood admiring the Salish Sea as it gently surged against Sechelt's foreshore. He had checked into the Boulevard Motel, popular for its seaside location and proximity to the town's centre. He'd be meeting with realtor Fred Vallevand, who said he had some suitable houses to look at.

Shortly after lunch, Brad went to Vallevand's office on nearby Teredo Street. It surprised him that the man with the big voice he had spoken to on the phone was shorter than average, with blond hair and smiling eyes.

What he lacked in size, he made up for with a cheerful can-do attitude.

"I've got four homes to show you," Vallevand said, "all of them good bets."

Brad soon learned that most homes near the shore were in a price category he wouldn't consider.

More importantly, they were often too much house for one person. After showing Brad three houses that didn't fully appeal to him, Vallevand said, "The next one should be exactly what you want. It just came on the market."

He then drove to a twenty-year-old, lap siding rancher. Its sixteen-hundred-square-feet featured two bedrooms, a den, one-and-one-half bathrooms, a two-car garage, a small, easy-care front yard, and a back patio bordering on a sensible-size lawn. Both sides of the property showed high, manicured shrubbery that added to privacy, something Brad appreciated.

The property's location on the high side of Marine Way provided the added bonus of a magnificent view of Porpoise Bay and Mount Richardson. It also had the convenience of being only a short drive to main street. The house showed quality and character, was a suitable size and at a price of about one-half the cost of a similar home in

Vancouver. He especially looked forward to enjoying the expansive water and mountain views that symbolized his escape from the “other” world to this natural and expansive environment that said “freedom.”

He learned from Vallevand that the neighbor on the left side was an elderly man who lived alone there. He spent many months away, apparently in Costa Rica. The elderly couple on the right kept pretty much to themselves. He’d meet them all eventually, but there would be no rush, especially until he got fully settled.

Two days later, he was in Vallevand’s office to complete the necessary paperwork. The home inspector had given the house a high mark, with no structural or operational problems. The purchase was further simplified by not requiring a mortgage. When he complimented Vallevand for his assistance, the compliment was returned, “Well, you made it easier for me than I’m used to. You impressed me with your ability to quickly size things up. You noticed even small things quickly. You might be surprised how long it takes some people to assess a home and decide if it's what they want."

Brad asked, "How long?"

Vallevand smiled, "A lot longer than it took you. You summed up its condition and value in the same light I did. Congratulations on an excellent purchase."

On Brad's first day in his new home, he stood at the front room's large bay window and gazed appreciatively at the view. He could see Porpoise Bay all the way to the opposite shore. The foreshore view took in the local marina, The Lighthouse building having a pub and restaurant.

He quickly became aware of the quiet that surrounded him. It reminded him of a conversation he had with his friend Jeffery over drinks at a pub shortly before he moved. Jeffery always enjoyed discussing philosophical social issues.

“You’re going to find things a whole lot quieter in Sechelt,” he said. “I've heard of people who are so used to the background hum and clatter of the city that they have difficulty sleeping without it … at least for a while. And Sechelt isn’t known for its dynamic lifestyle. You might even find it boring.”

Brad cocked his head. “That’s exactly why I’m going there. Not because it’s boring, but because of its more laid-back way of life that people like me find restful and encouraging to creativity. If you’ve ever walked in one of the area’s fantastic rainforests, you’ll know what I’m talking about—spirituality. The trees can be four feet and more in diameter, and reach more than a hundred feet into the air. They’re magnificent, with an aura that often encourages tree hugs. I always feel metaphysically inspired when walking among them.”

Jeffery snickered, “It’s the difference in the social scene that will take some getting used to. Lots of retired people. You’re going to want to meet someone to spend time with. It could take a long time to meet someone in your age bracket. The years may pass, but eventually you'll undoubtedly find a lovely senior lady to spend time with."

"Thanks. I've thought about all of that and have done some research on the town's demographics. I know it's a seniors' Valhalla, but I don't mean there are no people my age. At forty-nine, I'm below the town's median age bracket. I could very comfortably be with a woman in her late thirties with an age difference of ten or twelve years, a very common age difference anywhere. And there are many marriages with age differences of twenty years and more."

Jeffery agreed. "My girlfriend and I are nine years apart in age. Not that much different. Besides, it isn't just about age; it's about compatibility and that sort of thing, like having similar attraction and feelings."

"The woman I want should want the same things as me for a happy life together," Brad said.

"We'll be soulmates, think alike, feel alike, care alike – especially about each other. I know a married couple who say they're soulmates and described it as having levels of compatibility and emotions at an almost spiritual level." Brad had hoped he might find it on the Sunshine Coast, hopefully in Sechelt.

"Anyhow, Jeffery, I've always found it easy to meet people. I think what's most important initially is being involved in the fabric of the community and doing something meaningful. It can be many things, and for me, it should involve writing – writing for the media or whatever."

Jeffery was reminded of something he wanted to tell Brad. "Speaking of the media, there was a write-up in yesterday's Vancouver Sun about our friend Leonard Mason. He's being given bail after serving two years of the three they gave him. Can you believe it?"

Brad felt a jolt at the thought of Mason being released. "I'm not surprised with jail sentences these days. It's not something I'm going to worry about. He's the one who put himself there."

"Of course. You were only a witness."

"Right."

"But he could be a nuisance."

"I know he's vengeful and I'll keep an eye out for him."

Jeffery said, "Please do my friend. Even though he'll be under scrutiny, he may have learned some sneaky stuff inside."

Brad snickered. "Maybe I'll do some Google research and learn some sneaky counters to them. We'll see."

Though Brad was alone, he was in a world of possibilities. His biggest challenge would be to make something of his new lifestyle. What was important to him was having the dignity of employment. He wasn't someone who would watch TV all day, preferring instead to be almost preternaturally productive. He was like a firebrand that could be lit any time. The fuel was there; its format he'd tackle another day.

Brad had a busy first day in his new home, beginning with a tour to appraise what needed attention. He had previously arranged for an internet connection. He set up his office in the den, connected his computer, and got in touch with the world. His second tour appraised the interior colors. In his home-buying sallies, he had seen colors ranging from serene to serious.

He stood more in the serene camp, as had the sellers. The kitchen cabinets and counters were all beautifully harmonized in what could be called soothing and attractive earth tones, all showing good taste as did the walls and white ceiling. Kitchen appliances were relatively new. The front hallway and living room walls were a subtle blend of bone and tan. The main-floor bathroom showed a warm tone often seen in Mexico, a pleasant blend of tan with a light touch of orange.

The upper floor bedrooms showed a different mindset in colors, with pale green in one of them and mid-blue in the other. He visualized both rooms with something like bone or ivory, colors that go with almost everything. He'd hire painters to do the job. The den showed a pleasing tone of tan. He also liked its window that provided a view of tall trees and the bay as he sat at his desk.

The laundry room was a generous size and painted white. The well-used washer and dryer he might replace. The ensuite bathroom appeared particularly inviting, being off-white and completely renovated, with a large, attractive glassed-in shower and a glass doored medicine cabinet. He thought, I'll look forward to enjoying the shower before bed tonight. As for the rest of the house, it proved to be in move-in condition. Even the living room's Berber carpets, the tiled floors in the sweeping entranceway, kitchen, and bathroom looked as new.

There being no time to buy groceries, dinner

that night consisted of an ordered-in pizza. Later, after enjoying his new shower, Brad dug out some bedding and made up his bed near the wall furthest from the window that needed a sun blind. But Morpheus had no arms for him. Like other nights he thought about the shape of his future and the beginning of life without Karen. A big mistake. Always tired the next day.

Brad's early mornings in his new home were unlike any he'd previously experienced. His veil of sleep was parted by what sounded like aircraft on strafing runs passing overhead. Beginning at about seven-thirty, several aircraft began taking off from the float-plane base several blocks away. It'd be something he'd hear so often it'd simply become a momentary background sound: de Havilland Beaver float planes taking off with passengers bound to and from places like Vancouver, Sechelt, Nanaimo, and Victoria. He, of course, knew about Harbour Air's float-plane base on Porpoise Bay, but he hadn't before been in bed when the planes were leaving or flying home to roost. As the planes flew away, he again became aware of the quiet. Instead of Vancouver's heavy overcast of sounds, he heard a medley of bird songs, some of them new to him, a welcoming fresh tone on his first morning in his new home.

In the kitchen, a single portion of pizza reminded him that unless he could make do, there would be no breakfast, not even coffee. He quickly drove to Buccaneer's Restaurant several blocks away at the foot of Porpoise Bay and enjoyed a full breakfast while enjoying the panoramic view, the bay, the rain forests, and the mountains beyond. It felt good to be so well reminded of the wonderful natural landscape in the place he now called home. The rest of the morning was spent shopping for groceries and generally checking out the town to get a better sense of what it had to offer.

Downtown he found most things one would

expect in the retail sector. The area, known as Trail Bay Centre, boasts more than sixty stores, restaurants, and services of every kind. The flagship business is the popular family-owned Claytons Heritage Market, established in 1959 and still run by the family today. On the east side of town is Sechelt's other major shopping area, this one on Indian-band land. Tsain-Ko Village Shopping Centre has sixteen businesses of all kinds, some of them owned or operated by the Band or its members. Buildings throughout the center proudly display native wall carvings.

Brad learned that Sechelt Hospital across the street from the center is also on what had been Indian-band land. In 1964 the hospital acquired the 11.2 acres from the band for the sum of one dollar. Today, the large, modern, and well-equipped hospital includes a large helipad for medical helicopters transporting patients to and from Vancouver and elsewhere. On the same spread of land is Totem Lodge, a 49-bed long-term residential care facility providing 24-hour professional nursing services to people who are no longer able to safely live at home. Both the lodge and hospital show native pride in large, artistically carved totem poles.

Sechelt's location is unique, it being on an isthmus, its waist washed by Porpoise Bay on one side, the Salish Sea on the other, two alluring waterscapes that account for the town's name. Sechelt is the Caucasian spelling of the native Indian name, shíshálh, meaning "Land between two waters." He also learned the Sechelt Indian Band was the first in Canada to achieve self-governance, breaking away from the Indian Act in 1986. It gave them control over large areas of band land making its resources and services available to its members. On the nearby Salish Sea shore, Brad marveled at the several large and compelling totem poles that proudly proclaim 1986 self-governance and Sechelt Indian Band history.

Seeing the results of the Sechelt Indian Band's operating system was an eye-opener. Like other Indian Bands, it had pride in the community and a system that had served its population in a sustainable way for centuries. Examples of their purpose-driven methodologies can be seen today in the successes of their business models and governance.

After his first assessment of what the town had to offer, he planned to shop for basic food supplies. But first, he stopped for coffee at The Brew House, an inviting place with its coffee-colored paint tone and signage showing a cup being filled from a pot of coffee. As he stood at the counter, an attractive young woman turned and smiled, "Good morning, what can I get for you?"

"I'll have a long double espresso, please."

As she got his coffee, he noted what made her immediately attractive to his eye. Her shiny black hair had been cut in a style with bangs that emphasized her attractive facial features, including friendly eyes and an easy smile. She was taller than average, very fit, and perhaps in her late twenties or early thirties.

She placed the coffee in front of him. “I haven’t seen you before. Are you new in town?”

He smiled, amused. “Yes, I am. You’re pretty observant.”

“It’s how you’re dressed as much as anything. I can tell you’re from the city.” She held out her hand. “My name’s Adel.”

He took her hand. “Brad Webster.”

There being no other people wanting service, they had a short conversation during which he learned the coffee shop belonged to her widowed mother. Adel was the sole operator and would be until it became busier or she went back to Vancouver. She said she found Sechelt a bit on the quiet side. He could see that she was in every way very uptown, and little wonder she missed big-city buzz. He left the shop knowing it'd become a regular stop. Walking to his car, he thought, She's a sweet girl who could make a man wish he were younger – much younger.

Everything he had seen of Sechelt buoyed his spirits; it's where he belonged. There was a quality of life that inspired creative ambitions, as seen in the Coast's ever-burgeoning arts community. Driving home, he was high on expectations of good things to come, fired up to get more involved.

He'd no longer be distracted by the demands of the rat race that fed elsewhere. His move had been from static stress to dynamic new objectives, where change would be the byword; new appetites would be awakened, with time to feed them.

Chapter Six

After several days in his new home, the fact of his retirement quietly settled on Brad. He couldn't remember the last time he had no pressing demands. Now, with ample time to himself, he focused on household things needing attention. He had hired painters for both bedrooms; other things he did himself, such as installing new, stainless-steel, lever-type door handles on all doors and a new faucet in the downstairs half-bath.

The yard would be next. Something had to be done about those scruffy-looking dirt plots on each side of the patio. They were full of dried plants surrounded by what looked like old railway ties. It all had to come out and be replaced with pavers like the rest of the patio. Within a week, he had a hard-working young man from a local landscape company working on it. Matching pavers soon covered the entire patio, but it looked barren. It could be much improved with some flowering potted plants. At Home

Hardware, Brad bought two large decorative pots and set one on each side, after which they sat waiting for plants. The solution would lie with his daughter, Marie, who said she'd soon come to visit and see his new home. She always had a garden and lots of plants, and would, of course, know what to do. Meanwhile, he'd tidy up the front flower beds and replace a cracked paver on the walkway.

Three weeks later, Marie came with her dog, Preppy, a possessive and unfriendly male Chihuahua with itchy anal glands. It became apparent when, upon entering the house, he dragged his backside across the Berber carpet. Brad looked at Marie. “Did you see what he did?”

She calmly nodded, “Well, he’s got gland problems right now. Don’t worry, I've got something for it. And I‘ll give the carpet a wipe if it makes you feel better.”

“Alright, whatever you think will take care of it,” he said as calmly as he could.

They went to a couple of nurseries and found what she thought would be perfect for his pots. She chose chrysanthemums, generally appreciated for their range of colors in shades of red, yellow, white, orange, lavender, and purple flowers. He also bought a boxed set of plants that could be hung on the wooden fence. She said it'd pull everything together, and it did – more cozy and colorful from different angles.

Dinner that evening was at the Lighthouse Pub where they sat on the outside deck overlooking Porpoise Bay, taking in the furthest reaches to the mountains beyond. Marie enthused about the scene. "Dad, this is beautiful. I love the way you can see all the way down the inlet to the mountains. I bet you come here often."

"Only with friends and family. So keep it in mind and come often."

She laughed. "Good baiting. I'd like to, but I'm working and you're kind of on vacation. So don't forget where I live."

Preppy had, meanwhile, been left in Marie's car in the parking lot. "He'd go nuts if we left him at your house," she explained. "He's used to spending some time in my car, and he'll be alright while we have dinner. He knows I'll bring him a treat."

Over the course of the evening, they bantered good-naturedly as father and daughter, and—what they also enjoyed—as friends. They had a unique understanding and ability in dealing with politics-of-family interactions. It didn't have to be about role-playing. After discussing plants and the patio, she said she'd, on her next visit, give him some ideas about how the patio area could be made to look even better. Two months later, he still waited for another visit. He discovered that when one hints not to bring the dog, its owner mightn't come either, or would at least be slow to return. But he didn't think Marie would really be like that—or would she?

Brad often thought about the things to consider

in his day-to-day affairs. For example, when everything had fallen into place, and he had more free time, he aimed one day to become a part of the volunteer community. He'd get involved in fundraising for charities as he had done in Vancouver. If not this year, then the next.

He agreed with US President Ronald Reagan's statement: "We can't help everyone, but everyone can help someone." Brad couldn't have said it better. He especially wished to help needy seniors and would one day check out the appropriate social agencies. He also liked how Russia's Karl Marx so succinctly described helping someone: "From each according to his ability, to each according to his need." A little gem of humanity from an at times almost inhuman political philosophy.

Since moving to the Sunshine Coast, Brad had attended gatherings in various locations and found it difficult to find fellowship with men near his age in such things as hiking the many forest trails and exploring the backwoods. Then in a sporting goods store, he received information about two local hiking groups, one of them with morning hikes, the other in afternoons. The Ramblers sounded like a dynamic group; they hiked in the early afternoon, a better time for him than mornings, normally his best creative time. He contacted its leader, Chris Hansen, who invited him to join the group on their hike at Cliff Gilker Park the following Monday afternoon at 1:30 p.m. Perfect!

Monday dawned with a heavy overcast and light drizzle. In the parking lot, Brad joined the hikers who were mostly retired people, the reason they could hike during a weekday. There were six women and five men, one of them Chris, a tall blond-haired man who quickly approached. “You must be Brad. I’m glad you could make it. It should be a good day, even if there’s a bit of rain. You’ll hardly notice it in the forest. Today’s hike will cover a distance of about five kilometers. I don’t think it will be a problem for you." Chris also looked fit at about six feet in height and carrying no extra pounds. He walked lightly and stepped quickly as if raring to go. The sparkle in his blue eyes hinted at innate bonhomie. He looked to be in his forties. He called the group together, and they set off at an enthusiastic pace.

He soon joined Brad. "This is one of our more popular hikes, and it usually takes a little more than an hour." He eagerly told about highlights of the hike and whatever else could be of interest. Brad found Chris to be considerate, friendly, and communicative, the kind of person who was good company. He discovered Chris had been divorced for less than a year, had no children, was a partner in a Sechelt veterinary clinic, and took the time to hike for a few hours each week.

As the hike progressed, he gestured toward a waterfall that gurgled with moderate volume over a steep granite face. He pointed out that during spring runoff it flowed like a mini Niagara Falls, loudly cascading under a shroud of mist and into a stream that flowed to the Salish Sea

As they came to a bend in the path, a woman ahead of them suddenly screamed, “A snake,” and two women trotted back toward them. Chris held up his hand. “Wait a minute. What did the snake look like?”

A woman named Jessie, who seemed to be the most terrified, said, “I don’t know, but it looked mean, dark, almost black.”

Brad laughed. “I've read about it. It’s actually called the sharp-tailed snake and looks like a very small snake or a large worm. It’s harmless and actually has some color tints. Let’s go back and have a look.”

He led the way to where Jessie indicated she and another woman had seen it.

“There are no poisonous snakes in this part of BC,” he said. “I've checked it out, so don’t be alarmed.”

During the rest of the hike, the women kept a lookout for more snakes—just in case.

When the hikers returned to the parking lot, Chris asked Brad for his email address to keep him posted on upcoming hikes. It had been a good day in good company, and Brad looked forward to the next time. Given the park's features—the streams, majestic trees, berry bushes, varieties of fungi both good and bad, squirrels, chipmunks, birds, ferns, many varieties of plant life used for centuries by native people for health and pain relief—he knew he'd go there often.

On a warm, cloudy June afternoon, Brad set out to explore the hiking trail in Hidden Grove, a large tract of forest protected from logging by the citizen-initiated Sechelt Groves Society. As he drove down the narrow road north of Sechelt, he approached a small truck stopped by the roadside with its hood raised and a man bent under it. He stopped, put down his passenger-side window, and looked at the man.

“Everything okay?”

The man stood up. He was of medium height, solidly built, and had a large, grey mustache and friendly eyes. “It could be better. It's just quit on me.”

Brad pulled ahead to the side of the road and walked back. “Do you have any idea why it stopped?”

The man’s eyebrows and shoulders went up in unison as if attached. “I’m not sure. This morning when I started it, it began sputtering, but it smoothed out all right. Downtown it started doing it again, and it finally conked out here.”

Having long-time experience with car maintenance, Brad had a quick look at the engine and twisted the battery cables for tightness. “Sounds like it could be a dirty fuel problem or an electrical glitch. You’re not low on fuel?”

“I filled the tank yesterday.” He stood looking at the motor with his hands on his hips. “Well, it’s not going to get any better standing here.”

"Do you live near here?"

The man pointed. "I'm a few clicks up the road. No problem walking, and when I get home, I'll phone and have it towed to my mechanic."

"No need to walk, I'll drive you. I'm new in town and just exploring today. My name's Brad."

The man shook his hand, "Eric, and thanks for your help."

They soon arrived at a large, well-treed property, pleasingly rural. A neat-looking house anchored the end of a short driveway.

"I really appreciate your help," the man said. "You've got to come in and meet my misses."

As they approached the house, the door opened. "This is Brad," Eric said. "He came to my rescue when Chevy sputtered out on me. He's exploring today and was out for a drive."

"Well, aren't you lucky? Nice to meet you, Brad. I'm Connie." She was an attractive woman with wavy silver hair and a personality that shone with friendliness and warmth.

Eric ushered Brad into the house. “Come in, come in.” (he gestured to an armchair) “Have a seat. Would you join me for a drink?”

Brad thought for a moment. “All right.”

The home was older, yet remarkable for its decor and furnishings. Cupboards, hardwood floors, paint, all looked as if completed yesterday. The attractive wooden armchair Brad sat in looked like one of a kind, and unlike anything he had seen for its workmanship and colorful exotic wood.

“Someone did a nice job on this amazing chair.”

Connie smiled. “You’re looking at him. Eric did all of our woodwork. I did most of the interior painting.”

“I'd have used less yellow,” quipped Eric from the kitchen.

Connie pointed to the kitchen wall. “It’s not

yellow, it's canary. Anybody can have yellow."

"We can't get away from our favorites. And I'm going to pour us one of my favorites, ouzo," said Eric. "Have you tried it?"

Brad nodded. "Yes, in Greece I attended a dinner party where they drank lots of ouzo. I liked Greece, the people, the food, the music, but I discovered you have to go easy with ouzo."

Eric laughed in agreement. "It's something you learn to do. I'm of Greek heritage, born in Canada. We've been back to Greece several times. I have cousins there."

In the kitchen, he phoned the tow truck operator and poured drinks. He looked at Connie. She shook her head.

"Brad, do you like water or ice with your drink?"

"Thanks. I'll take mine with a bit of water."

He returned with two glasses of ouzo and a cream pitcher of water and placed them on the coffee table.

"The tow truck will come shortly. I told him I put the key under the floor mat." He laughed, "I guess I could have left it in the ignition." He raised his glass, "Opa."

Eric and Connie were genuinely interested in Brad, who he was, where he was from, what he did, was he married, if not why not, 'a good-looking guy like you' and what brought him to Sechelt. An hour quickly sped by, and Brad looked at his watch. "Well, folks, I'm going to say goodbye and check out the Hidden Grove hiking trail. I've enjoyed our time and I hope to see you again soon."

"You know where we live, so by all means drop by anytime," Connie said.

At the door, Eric said, "Our number's in the phone book. Last name's Megalos ... spelled just the way it sounds. So don't hesitate to give us a call."

Brad pulled onto the road thinking about how much he enjoyed the Megalos. Nice people. I'll definitely see them again. He noted that the sky had darkened, and it was beginning to sprinkle. He decided to check out the hiking trail another day. He drove home paying more attention to cars in his rearview mirror. A new habit.

Chapter Seven

Brad had always been an avid book reader and became a regular visitor to the Sechelt library. He also checked out thrift store book shelves where he'd buy a book for a dollar or two, read it, and return it. He especially looked for favorite authors and book covers with the line "New York Times Best Selling Author." While browsing in Sechelt's Health Care Auxiliary Thrift Store, he one day noticed an attractive middle-aged woman sitting on a chair holding a large coffee-table book. She looked up at him, and something in her gaze drew him nearer.

Seeing the word "Mexico" on the book's cover, he said, "I'm guessing you have an interest in Mexico, one of my favorite places."

The woman stood up – she was tall, slim, and attractive – and placed the book on a shelf. "It's one of my favorite places, too," she said, turning to face him. "Do you know it well?" Brad asked.

She smiled. “Yes. I’m having a home built there.”

“I've been to many parts of Mexico. Can I ask where it will be?”

“Lake Chapala. Have you been there?”

“Yes. And I have a friend who lives not far from Ajijic.”

Her face lit up in a smile, and her large, dark-brown eyes gleamed happily. The subject was clearly enticing. Brad introduced himself, adding, “I've met many Canadians in Mexico who are very happy living there.”

“I’m Alexis Robertson, and yes, I am looking forward to living there, too. I’m renting a condo here until my home’s built. I moved here from Victoria because my sister moved here, and we can enjoy some time together.”

They were soon in a lively conversation, and after exchanging a few more specifics about living in

Mexico, Alexis said, “I’m going across the street for coffee. If you care to join me, we could talk more about what appears to be one of our favorite subjects.”

Over coffee, Alexis told him about her Mexican home. It featured a well-equipped kitchen, two bedrooms, a bathroom, a den, and a patio overlooking Lake Chapala from which the town is named. Brad quickly found himself in a discussion about Mexico and experiences while at the same time enjoying this beguiling woman. “Your place sounds nice, and I know it’s a great area for retirement. I’d still like to see more of Mexico. I enjoy the people and communicating with them.”

Alexis had a sip of coffee, studying him over the cup’s rim. “You’ve spent a lot of time in Mexico, and you obviously speak Spanish. No wonder you’re so comfortable there.” “It’s a great language, except maybe the verbs, transitive, intransitive, reflexive. (he laughed) “But there are ways to get around most of it. How about you?"

"Well, I'm learning Spanish the slow way with what I've picked up here and there and on internet translation sites. I've also taken a few lessons. I can make myself understood quite well sometimes and can understand a lot of Spanish if spoken despacio."

"Meaning slowly, and you said it very well. You say you have a sister living here?" "I do. She moved here from Vancouver in February. Call it a new beginning."

"I sense a story here, an escape from this or that," he said. "Is she younger or older than you?"

She looked at him and smiled. "She's younger." "Was she able to find a meaningful job?"

"You ask a lot of questions. What do you do?"

He laughed. "I'm between jobs. I've retired from the nine-to-five lifestyle, at least for now. I owned a Vancouver publishing business and had to ask a lot of questions to get the full story, the who, what, when, where, and why. People have at times told me it sounds like I'm interviewing them. But these days it's because I'm simply interested in who they are."

She smiled and suddenly became philosophical. "Building a home in Mexico or any foreign country can be a bit daunting, but it's where I want to live out my life. At least that's how I feel now. What about you? Where do you expect to live out your life?"

He had a sip of coffee. "I'd have to think about that. There can be many turns in the road. But I admire you for taking that road and seeing if it leads to where you wish to remain." He had been taken aback by her question. He had never before been asked where he'd wish to live out his life, certainly not with real interest. Her questions were like he, too, was being interviewed, and quite aggressively, too.

He put down his cup. "I've been to Mexico several times, and I've always enjoyed it. I've also traveled around the world and have seen many beautiful places, but I have to say I love this country, this province, and especially this beautiful Sunshine Coast. As to where else to live? At this moment, I can't think beyond being right here, and it keeps showing me reasons to stay."

She wasn't letting him off easily. "But wouldn't you like to have another venue in which to spend time, especially in the winter?"

"Of course. I've always found Mexico a great place to go in the winter, or whenever I feel influenced by wanderlust."

"Well, there you go. I'll have to tell you more about the community I'm moving to. It might sound lonely going there by myself, but it's an expat community full of Canadians and Americans, some of them married and others single like me. I met many of them when arranging for the purchase of my property."

He raised an eyebrow. "But you like Mexican people, too, I'd expect."

She nodded enthusiastically. “Yes, very much. I love interacting with them.” (She laughed) “And practicing my Spanish.”

As their repartee flowed, it felt reassuring to be so quickly in tune with an attractive and interesting woman like Alexis. Before leaving the coffee shop, she gave him her phone number, and they agreed to meet again soon.

At home during lunch, he thought back on their meeting, how she seemed classy, confident, enthusiastic, and wonderfully adept at influencing a budding friendship. Since arriving in Sechelt, it had been his first occasion to spend time with such an interesting woman – actually, any woman. He cheered and looked forward to seeing her again.

They had met on Tuesday, and on Friday, he thought about the weekend and how it'd be a waste of social amenity not to include Alexis in his agenda. He decided to phone and ask her out to dinner. She told him her social calendar was without commitments and she'd be delighted to go to dinner with him.

On Saturday at five o'clock, he was at her place for her offered pre-dinner drink. Her coffee table was set out with a bottle of tequila, glasses, pitchers of ice and water, and some taco chips.

He chuckled. "So you like tequila, too."

"Well, yes, I do like it, as should anyone wishing to live in Mexico."

She looked stunning in a navy-blue, patterned dress. He saw again what attracted him when he first met her: her poise and confidence, her intelligence, the warmth seen in her eyes and her attractively styled shoulder-length brunette hair.

"You look great," he enthused. "But as I said on the phone, we're only going to the Lighthouse Pub."

She smiled. "I know, but I enjoy a table on the deck and seeing the wonderful view." (She gestured to the sofa) "The food's good, too. And, by the way, you also look nice."

They sat on the sofa, and she poured tequila into two glasses. She looked at him. "Ice?"

He nodded.

"Water?"

He nodded again, with thumb and forefinger indicating a small amount.

She put on some music that hinted at Latin sensibilities. "I love this music; it's so nice to dance to. Do you like to dance?"

He stood up, reached for her hand, and quickly led her in a smooth two-step.

"You're a great dancer," she said as they returned to the sofa, both of them buoyed by the contact.

"So are you. I really enjoyed that."

"My sister's a better dancer. She studied ballet."

"So I take it you didn't."

"No, I studied nursing, and that's how I met my husband David. He was a doctor. I lost him two years ago to pancreatic cancer. Until that happened, we had some good times in Mexico." (She paused) "Let's have another drink before we go, and you can tell me more about you."

As she poured their drinks, he looked at a framed photo on the wall above the sofa. Two women sat at a table under a large umbrella. The surroundings and colors looked exotic, with an ocean and its limitless horizon filling the background.

He studied it for a moment. "I see you in the photo, but who is the other woman?"

"That's my sister Meagan. We were having lunch at our hotel in Puerto Vallarta."

He continued to gaze at the photo. She's beautiful.

At the pub, they sat at a table on the deck

enjoying the broad view of Porpoise Bay. As Alexis took in the scene, she suddenly grasped Brad's hand. "There's an eagle in that tree," she said, pointing. "One time when Meagan and I were here, we saw an eagle sweep low over the water, undoubtedly looking for a fish."

"We're seeing nature at work," he said. "Being in the natural environment is one of the joys of being here. I wanted to be near the water, and if you look high up at about the middle of the wharf, you can see my rooftop. I never get tired of looking at the view. In fact, it's the first thing I look at in the morning."

"Maybe I can see your home someday."

"Maybe tomorrow if you wish."

"I can't tomorrow. I'm helping my sister do some painting."

She leaned back as the server brought their drink order. "And her place also needs a bit of fixing up."

Brad cocked his head. “Well, fixing things isn’t a brutally demanding skill, and it’s something I've always done in my home.”

“Maybe you could have a look at her place sometime and point out things that need to be fixed.” She looked at him with a raised eyebrow.

“And how to do it.”

He put down his drink. “I’m not doing anything tomorrow. I’d be glad to lend a hand.”

“I wouldn’t have asked you.”

“You didn’t have to.” He smiled. “I got the message.”

She raised her glass. “It’s a deal then. Cheers.”

“A deal it is. Cheers.”

“We’ll be meeting at ten o’clock. Meagan’s address is 750 Crayfish Avenue.” She reached into her purse and wrote on the back of someone’s business card. “I’ll look forward to seeing you, and you don’t have to be there at ten.”

"No problem." He peered at her over his menu. "Have you decided what you'd like for dinner? I can vouch for the salmon. I'm going to have ribs. They're always good, too."

"I think I will have the salmon. The last time I was here with Meagan, I had the ribs. Yes, they were good, but I think it's nice to have two favorites."

He gazed at her, seeing a woman confident and strong-willed, a woman whom he thought would be very decided on relationship matters. Her company felt good, and he looked forward to knowing her better.

"Tell me more about your Mexican home's anticipated features. I've seen some of them built for Canadian friends, and I'm always impressed by the attractive construction details, especially interior elements like arched doorways and terrazzo floors."

She sat back. "I'm going to have it built by local builders who were recommended to me by some of the expats I met there. As I pointed out before, it will be a decent size, with two bedrooms, and I'll have a sundeck with a view of the lake."

"It sounds nice."

"Things are moving slowly. The purchase has been agreed to, and I have a lawyer working on the final paperwork as we speak. But, as you may know, there's often no rush about some things in Mexico. They don't believe in doing things at breakneck speed, as we sometimes do. When it's built, it'll have lots of room, and you can come to visit."

He thought for a moment, "I'll definitely keep it in mind."

While waiting for dinner to be served, he excused himself to go to the washroom. As he returned to the table, he glanced at a man who sat at the bar gazing at him. He kept walking and thought, is that Mason? He stopped for a better look – it wasn't Mason. Damn it, he thought, I shouldn't be thinking about something so remote. He'd have to get permission from his parole officer to leave town and say where he was going. That would provide an element of security by knowing where he was headed. He continued to the table determined not to mention anything about it.

After dinner, he dropped Alexis off at her apartment and thought about how he felt after being out with her. As he drove home, checking his rearview mirror, he didn’t anticipate that he and she would be more than friends. Since his divorce, and before he met Karen, his involvement with women never got past the early-romance stage because he hadn't felt the need to marry again or even live together – at least not yet. To further complicate matters, his love interests were invariably younger women who did want to get married and start a family. His unshakable stance had been the death knell to his romances.

Since his breakup with Karen, he hadn’t taken the time to explore the what-ifs: what if he met a woman closer to his age, what if they struck up a more realistic relationship wanting the same things, to remain together and even marry? He hadn't seriously dwelled on his prospects of meeting a woman he might seriously consider marrying, a woman who was older. At least not until he met Alexis. Even though the having children part wouldn't be a factor, the concept seemed a long shot. He knew nothing of her innermost feelings or any of the other things that make someone truly knowable in a meaningful way. And what if something did come of it, and he was on the periphery of something truly meaningful? But she was moving to Mexico. He thought, *Well,* I like Mexico too.

Chapter Eight

On Sunday morning, Brad arrived at Meagan's house a few minutes before ten o'clock. The small house looked much like the others on the street, six post-war houses, all of a similar size. What were once summer cottages for city folk were now practical, updated homes. While some of them were in need of paint, Meagan's house sported a fresh tone of tan, with chocolate trim and shutters, an attractive cachet setting it apart. As he walked to the front door, he felt a sense of expectation in meeting Meagan. He stifled a laugh when, looking through the open door, he saw Alexis dressed in blue jeans, a flannel shirt, and runners.

"Is this the same woman I had dinner with last night?"

She spun around. "I'm showing my other side, the one that gets the job done. In fact, you look a bit overdressed for this sort of work. I'm not sure those expensive shoes would look as good with paint on them."

"Today, I thought I'd be the taper and fixer. I brought some tape that will keep the paint off the ceiling and trim for a neater looking job."

As they chatted, a tall, strikingly beautiful woman walked into the room wearing a T-shirt, shorts, and runners as if going to a beach. Alexis turned to her. "Meagan, come and meet Brad."

Her honey-blonde hair, pulled back in a ponytail, revealed a beautiful oval-shaped face and large, hazel eyes, features that showed a woman with beauty to spare. But it wasn't only her beauty that piqued Brad's senses. It was her demeanor, the way she walked and her warm smile. She now stood there like the sudden appearance of someone he had dreamed about or at least thought about, someone truly special.

Alexis gestured. "This is my sister Meagan." (gesturing again) "This is Brad, my thrift store bargain."

She offered her hand, smiling. "Nice to meet you, Brad."

He took her hand. “Hi Meagan, nice to meet you, too. By the way, I wasn’t in the bargain section.”

As the three of them shared a laugh and some light conversation, Meagan and Brad each took every opportunity to appraise the other. Meagan epitomized the kind of woman he had hoped to meet, and here she was, like manifest destiny. It didn’t seem possible. Meagan had similar feelings about Brad’s attributes; they were unlike any she had seen since moving to Sechelt in February.

Moments later, Alexis gestured to a desultory-looking man leaning against the wall. “This is Meagan’s neighbor, Will. He has offered to give us a hand today. He helped me a while ago, too.”

Will nudged himself from the wall and shook hands with Brad, who couldn’t help noticing his demeanor that might've been annoyance at the upset of the male balance. Will appeared to be in his early forties, with unruly black hair and an obviously broken nose looking slightly askew. He rented one of the houses further down the street. Since Meagan bought her house, he'd developed a fixation about her. Being on the outward curve of the road, he could see the front half of her house, and he never tired of seeing her comings and goings, admiring her beauty and grace. He wanted to get to know her better, but she kept to herself. His first opportunity to use some initiative in the matter occurred on a day he had walked by Meagan's house as she was changing the bulb in her porch light.

He stopped, looked at her and said, "Your stool looks a bit unsteady. Can I give you a hand? I live over there. (he pointed) My name's Will."

Meagan shakily stepped off the stool. "Oh, hi. Yes, I was having some trouble getting the bulb out. It seems a bit stuck."

He walked over, reset the stool, and removed the burned-out bulb, noting the badly rusted light fixture.

"It's no wonder you were having trouble. The

fixture is badly corroded. I've one at home I recently replaced, and it looks a lot better than this one. I'll be right back." After fetching it, he gave it a few wipes and installed it with Meagan's new bulb.

Looking at it appraisingly, she said, "Well, that certainly looks a lot better. Thank you very much, Will."

Since then, he hadn't had another opportunity to speak with her. And it wouldn't have happened this time if he hadn't walked by as she unloaded paint cans and supplies. When he said he had good painting experience, she accepted his help.

Brad couldn't help noticing Will's fawning attention, and he wondered if either woman would reflect some of the same interest in Will. He sensed it wouldn't be Meagan. Whether or not she accepted Will beyond neighborly friendliness wasn't evident, but he certainly showed obvious interest in both of the sisters.

Alexis had been anticipating the day and felt

eager to apply herself to the task. “We’ll find out who knows how to paint today. I can’t say I’m great, but I’m willing and able.”

The day’s objective would be to paint the bedroom and bathroom walls pale blue. Meagan had purchased everything she thought would be needed, including pizza and chocolate cake.

Alexis put up her hand. “Who's going to be project boss? There has to be someone at the rudder to steer us from disaster.”

Brad would have volunteered, but Will quickly spoke up.

“I’ll do it unless you want to, Meagan. It’s your place.”

“No, I don’t know enough about this sort of thing.” She turned to Brad.

“Maybe you’d also like to be boss.”

He shook his head. “One boss is enough. And I’m not a great painter either. I always hire painters.

I'll do the taping if that's alright with you, Will."

His comment drew a hard look from Will who threw up his hands with an affirmative grunt.

"I knew I might be forgetting something." Meagan stood with her hands on her hips. "I never even thought about painter's tape. Thanks, Brad."

He smiled reassuringly, "Nothing to worry about. I brought lots, so I'll get to work on it."

As he did the taping, he thought about the odds of meeting Meagan here and now. If she's the kind of woman I think she is, it seems too good to be true – her personality, her age. I need to find out who she really is. He put it in the back of his mind, finished the taping, and began looking for things that needed fixing. As he scanned the living room, he couldn't help admiring some of Meagan's attractive furnishings. Bookcase shelves had several titles Brad had read. He saw Thomas Hardy's titles – 'The Mayor of Casterbridge' and 'Tess of the d'Urbervilles' – two that he had particularly enjoyed. There were also books of poetry, from Burns to Wordsworth. Obviously an avid reader, she was becoming more interesting by the minute.

As he continued scanning the rooms, he noted some things that might not be noticeable to someone who had never done household repairs. Across the room, he saw Meagan standing with a paint roller in her hand while looking at a bathroom wall. He stood looking at her absorbingly, struck by her enticing aura. She turned, sensing him. “Are you finding anything seriously wrong?”

“I won’t know until I have a good look around and make my report.”

“Could there be really bad things?”

“Not really bad. Nothing we can’t fix.”

She frowned fawningly. “We? I don’t know much about repairing things.” He snickered. “Don’t worry about it. If you give me some paper and a pen, I’ll jot down some things to discuss with you.” As he toured the house, the list grew, especially in the kitchen: loose hinges on most cupboard doors, the faucet dripped and would probably need a new O-ring.

Further checking revealed a wall with an electrical outlet further back than the wall's surface because it wasn't properly screwed to the stud, leaving the plastic faceplate hanging loosely. And the kitchen floor had some badly cracked vinyl tile. Not a lot, but it definitely needed some replacing. Wasting no time, he went to his car and returned with his toolbox. He first attached the loose plug-in to the stud so it'd be flush with the wall, and he then tightened the plastic faceplate. Later, as he firmed up hinges on cupboard doors, he didn't see Meagan standing back and appraising him from top to bottom and liking what she saw: a very fit man who didn't hesitate to help out and do it well. The other side of him she liked, too. She found him attractive, personable, and very masculine.

An hour later, seeing him standing in the

kitchen surveying the cabinets, she said, "How's the list shaping up? Will it send me to the poor house?"

He turned and smiled at her. "Let's just say that you won't be put in dire straits. Most of your cabinet doors sag a bit because the hinges have serious arthritis. They should be replaced. It's all doable."

She looked deeply into his eyes. "I'll appreciate whatever you can do."

Her eyes by now had become mesmerizing and, as they held onto his, he felt a surge of attraction. He held his breath for a moment, "No problem, they're things I've done before and are well worth doing, like polishing something valuable."

"Very apt … I like that. Are you ready for a coffee?"

"I didn't think I'd worked that hard yet."

"We treat our workers very well here."

He chuckled. "Sounds good."

She started making coffee, getting slightly

flushed as Brad stood near her.

"So, Meagan, how long have you had the house?"

"I bought it in February from an old lady who had lived here for, I think, she said twenty-three years. And you can tell she didn't do much to it, probably couldn't afford to. It's going to be awhile before I can get things looking the way I want them. The good thing is I've got a job working for my long-time Vancouver friend Cindy, who moved here last year and started a women's clothing and shoe store. She's done a great job of fixing it up and stocking it more or less city style. The store has been open for almost a year and is doing well.

When she heard of my divorce, she asked me if I'd be interested in working with her, with a possible future buy-in. So I made the decision, a big decision, to sell my condo and move here. Alexis made it easier for me when she said she'd move here, too, and rent a place while her Mexican house is being built. It meant we could see each other for a few months."

"So how are you feeling about things now?"

"I'm happy with the move," she said, reaching for cups in the cupboard. "Another reason I came here is because I like the Sunshine Coast. It's a nice change, so scenic and restful. I needed a change from everything. And what about you?"

Seeing her difficulty in reaching cups at the back of the shelf, he stepped closer to her and reached for them. He placed his other hand on her shoulder for balance and immediately felt her essence and warmth, like an enticing current.

He hesitated before continuing. "My motivations are in some ways similar to yours, an escape from the past. The Sunshine Coast lifestyle beckoned to me after years of doing business in Vancouver. I owned a magazine, and this year I felt the time was right to sell it and go for early retirement. So I sold it and my house and bought a place near

Porpoise Bay a couple of months ago. I wanted to be near the water. And while I have a grown son and daughter, and friends in Vancouver, they're only forty minutes away by ferry. So what about you, do you have children?"

She glanced at him. "No, it wasn't meant to happen. Fate had other plans for me." She momentarily changed the subject saying, "Thanks for getting the cups down. That shelf's a bit high … so when I came here I had been divorced for almost a year and happy to be in my own home alone. Here I was at age thirty-nine, divorced and starting all over again. I'm probably too independent."

"I'm independent, but you don't strike me as being too independent. If a shrink's couch was handy, we could get to the bottom of this … take turns."

She giggled. "You first."

He smiled. "No problem." and gazed out the window at the house next door. "Have you met your neighbors yet?"

“That one belongs to Emily Folger, an elderly widow and longtime resident. I don’t see her much, but she seems nice. And on the other side is an old bachelor named Ollie Sigurdson. He works on a trawler in the North Pacific for half the year and vacations in Mexico the rest of the time. I've seen him twice.”

“Hey, what are you two up to?” Alexis stood with a paint roller in her hand; her other hand held a paper towel under a drip. “I thought we were supposed to be working.”

“I have to finish one wall,” Meagan smiled brightly. “And I've made coffee, so it’s here when anyone wants it.”

“We’re not even half finished, but let’s see if some java livens us up,” Alexis said. “Will, come and have some coffee.”

He poked his head around a corner. “So this is where everyone disappeared to.”

Meagan laid out cups, cream, and sugar and began pouring coffee. She looked at Alexis. “Brad’s made a fix-it list for things needing repair.”

“Repair is part of the joy of homeownership,” Alexis opined. “Especially if it’s an older home.” She looked at Brad. “Is any of it serious?”

“Nothing’s so bad that it can’t be fixed or made better with simple tools.”

“Sounds like you like fixing things.”

“I enjoy making things work better and look better. Whether it’s a house or a car, I've always done repairs of all kinds.”

“That’s something I do, too,” Will interjected.

Alexis spoke up. “Will’s an electrician. He fixed one of my lamps and then replaced a sensor on my SUV.”

Meagan looked at her, surprised, and said, “How interesting.” “I replaced some sensors on my last car,” Brad put in.

"Oh yeah, which ones?" said Will, challengingly.

Brad said, "The mass airflow sensor and the low coolant sensor, neither of them particularly difficult. The airflow sensor was the easiest. Removal and replacement took about thirty minutes and saved at least one hundred dollars."

"I could have done it quicker than that," Will said with a smirk.

Meagan wisely thought to change the subject. "I'm going back to work."

Everyone finished their coffees and was soon back on the job. Brad continued working on the cupboard doors until they lined up evenly in spite of loose hinges. He looked at them thinking, I'll talk to Meagan about replacing them and, hopefully, get to know her.

Later, Meagan returned to the kitchen where the faucet lay in several pieces on the counter. She stood looking at them and turned to Brad.

"I was going to have a glass of water, but no problem, I'll get it in the bathroom. Is it anything serious?"

"Well, I thought it'd be a simple O-ring problem and it is. I'll put it back together and get you a new ring."

She raised an eyebrow. "How many carats?"

Brad snickered. "For you, it'll be huge. I might have to shop around, or even go to Vancouver to get it."

She flushed, realizing her question sounded more familiar than intended. She cooled the moment with a quick look at the clock. "Are you ready for some pizza? They have scrumptious toppings, black olives and slivered garlic, and I like to add sliced tomatoes. I think you'll like it. I've got three large pizzas and a chocolate cake for dessert."

"It sounds like a delicious energy lunch. Can I

help with anything?"

She pointed. "You can slice those tomatoes. You'll have to wash them first."

He nodded. "My grandmother always used to say, 'Wash this and that, get rid of the germs.' It became automatic, and I washed everything."

"I'm the same way," she said. "It makes sense, especially when coming home after being out and touching this and that. I don't think we're germaphobes, are we?"

He chuckled, "Maybe."

They both laughed at their supposed sensibilities. "So how many tomatoes?"

"Three should be enough and not sliced too thick," she suggested. "You be the judge. After you've placed them evenly on top, I'll pop the pizzas in the oven." She turned and smiled at him appreciatively, "Thank you for your help, Brad."

He held her gaze. "Anytime, Meagan. I'm

always glad to help out."

She watched him carefully wash the tomatoes and dry them with a paper towel, feeling attachment to him. She thought about how she had never had a man be so willingly helpful and capable. And he communicated in such a wonderful way – the sound of his voice. As she watched him carefully slicing the tomatoes, she felt a sudden urge to wrap him in her arms.

Chapter Nine

As Brad finished slicing the tomatoes, Alexis looked in. “What delicious-looking pizzas. They make me realize I’m starving.”

“And you probably thought you were the only ones working,” he said, rinsing and drying his hands.

“We were wondering, and also when lunch was going to be served. But Will and I are a good team, and we decided to power on. Meagan, you said the ceiling will be okay as is, but now with the walls done up, it’s looking like it could use some cleaning or painting.”

Meagan waved a hand at it. “It might simply need some wet wiping. I’ll try that in a couple of days, and if it doesn't look better, we’ll have to paint it.”

Alexis looked at her with arched eyebrows. “We will, will we?”

Meagan shook her head. “I’m not going to worry about it now. I’ll wait for the paint muse to tell me when the time is right."

When the pizzas were out of the oven, Meagan called everyone to the kitchen. It being small, Brad and Meagan contentedly stood near each other at the counter. Alexis and Will sat at the table. Pizzas and chocolate cake quickly disappeared. Everyone agreed it was a delicious windup for work done. With contented murmurs and some generalizations about what newly acquired homes often require, lunchtime ended. Alexis and Will soon left, heading out in opposite directions.

Brad gathered up his tools, thanked Meagan for lunch, and said, "I'll pick up the parts we'll need, including several new hinges for your cupboards, so"

"They can't be too expensive. Should we not replace them all?"

"I think we should." He looked at the cupboards. "There's eight doors on top and six below. Two hinges per door, I'll pick up twenty-eight."

"Thank you so much, Brad. And be sure to give me the receipt."

He turned to leave. "If you give me your phone number, we can set up a time to have the parts installed."

She wrote it on a piece of paper and thought about putting a heart on it, but decided not to before handing it to him. It wasn't the right time. As he went out the door, she followed him, wishing he could have stayed longer.

"I really appreciate your help, Brad. I'm so glad you came."

As he opened his car door, she approached and stood with her hand on the driver-side front fender. He couldn't help being once again struck by her beauty, her essence. She appeared to be about five-foot-nine or ten in height, with a figure that seemed to be the result of either genetics or attention to fitness, or both. Everything in her comportment, from her proud posture and the way she walked, with a graceful spring in her step, showed more pride than vanity, making her even more exceptional in his eyes. He looked at her wanting to say more than merely saying goodbye.

"Meagan, I enjoyed helping out today. There are a few more things that should be done, and at very little cost. I can point them out to you next time I see you … when I install the hinges and O-ring."

"I'll look forward to it. We'll have a coffee chat and get to know more about each other."

Brad snickered. "Not necessarily confessional."

She giggled. "Come on, we won't tell anyone."

He got into his car, almost sitting on his toolbox, and waved as he drove away. On his way home, he couldn't help thinking about how when communicating with Meagan, she spoke in such an easy and fundamental way, a way that had a mercurial effect on him. She also seemed tantalizingly enigmatic, as if biding her time before fully revealing much about herself, in sharp contrast to Alexis. Since his breakup with Karen, he had many times thought about the important elements in a relationship, and it wasn't all about appearances. Meagan had opened his eyes to traits he instinctively knew were near the top of the list: good communication, intelligence, sincerity, and humor – good soulmate qualities, he thought. She had these as well as innate warmth and friendliness. As he drove thinking about her, his press of feelings brought to mind a favorite quote, what must have been a similar feeling felt by poet Robert Browning when he wrote: "She should never have looked at me if she meant I should not love her."

On Monday morning, Brad discovered that his clothes dryer took forever to dry a load of towels or anything else with extra weight to it. In his previous home, having a similar drying problem, he installed a new heating element. This one shouldn't be much different, though he had some doubts about its overall condition. He got his toolbox, and minutes later stood looking into the bowels of the dryer. It wasn't at all like his other one; this one would be a difficult fix. The washing machine, too, had seen better days. It became a no-brainer: the best way to fix the problem would be to buy a new set.

On Tuesday, he drove to the town's Sears store to see what they had in washer and dryer models. On Wednesday, he'd also do some comparison shopping at The Brick in Gibsons, only a twenty-minute drive east of Sechelt. He'd like to invite Meagan, show her around and get to know her better, but she has a job. Maybe Alexis would like to go along. As it turned out, she had nothing planned for the day and happily accepted his invitation and the inducement of lunch at the iconic Molly's Reach Restaurant on Gibsons' waterfront.

On Wednesday morning, he felt cheered as he drove to Alexis' home at eleven o'clock. It'd be a pleasant change to have someone accompany him on a shopping trip out of town. As they were leaving Sechelt, she put her hand on his knee. “I’m so glad you invited me along. There isn’t always something here to occupy me in a way that is either meaningful or interesting. Waiting for my house to be built is keeping me in a frustrating holding mode. I’m sure you understand.”

He nodded encouragingly. “Simply putting in time can be challenging. But at least you have Meagan you can do things with to help pass the time. I could imagine the two of you going on happy shopping sprees or just window-shopping. And if not here, then catch a ferry to Vancouver and really go to town.”

“But that’s all rather expensive. And with my moving to Mexico, there’s only so much I want to accumulate before going there. I’ll sell my larger items and ship the rest. Of course, I’ll take my personal and more valuable items with me. You realize, of course, I’ll be driving my SUV to Mexico.

But I can't help being concerned about shipping things and hoping they'll reach me."

"And driving there alone seems like enough of a challenge for anyone. Have you ever driven there before?"

"Oh yes, I drove there to search for the property I wanted to build on. Besides, I enjoy driving and seeing new places."

"I like Mexico, too, and I've been there many times. As I've mentioned, I have a friend living in nearby Ajijic whom I've visited a couple of times."

"When my home's built, you'll have to come down and visit me sometime. There'll be lots of room, two bedrooms, both with locks on the doors." (She laughed) "You'll be safe."

He couldn't help chuckling at her implication. It wasn't until she said it that he began to get a clearer picture of her agenda. If I did lock it, she'd probably be upset, he thought, and an unlocked door could have some interesting possibilities.

He stopped thinking about it, saying, "What's your best guess as to when it will be completed? What are you hoping for?"

"Well, nothing's going to really get started until the foundation is poured. But before that happens, some final paperwork has to be completed. I expect to hear from my lawyer soon. Then I'll return the signed papers, with a check. It's a bit frustrating, but all very exciting. I'm buying the property from a Canadian widow who lives on the lot beside it. As far as building my house is concerned, friends have recommended a construction foreman, a man named Miguel, who can pull the workers together and get on with the job. My friends have been a great help with finding resources."

"Have there been any problems?"

She thought for a moment. "Not really, other than the fact that many Canadians and Americans are buying properties down there, and finding available workers is becoming a challenge."

"Well, if you're there at Christmas, and I've been there at Christmas, I know you'll have a bang-up time. They really know how to celebrate fiestas of all kinds. And to hell with the neighbors. A Mexican couple once invited me to a party that flowed out from the house into the backyard and became quite noisy. I asked the homeowner if his neighbors would mind. His response: 'No, because they know they can also have their parties without me complaining.'"

"A case of live and let live," Brad had said.

The man nodded. "The Mexican way."

Alexis waved her hand. "Well that's fine and good until the time you want a good night's sleep and the neighbor's noise makes it impossible. I once stayed at a place where roosters woke me before daylight. I don't know which would be worse. Fortunately, my home's in a community with lots of Canadians and Americans, and few roosters, if any."

As she continued, he noticed a car behind him that had been there since they passed Robert's Creek. Here it comes. As it passed, he was relieved to see it driven by a woman. I've got to stop doing this. He hasn't even been released yet.

Arriving at The Brick, he quickly homed in on washers and dryers and purchased a GE set touted as "Commercial Quality." Brad felt it was a bargain selling at nearly the same price as standard sets he'd previously seen. It'd be delivered in two days.

Lunchtime saw them at Molly's Reach Restaurant, pleasingly situated beside Gibsons Marina, where diners can see the marina's vast panorama of boats of all types and sizes. Brad had learned the restaurant name is a carryover from the CBC's comedy-drama television series The Beachcombers that ran from October 1972 to December 1990, the story being centered in Gibsons. Molly's Reach was the name of the café owned by the character Molly Carmody. They enjoyed a delicious lunch that was every bit as good as the restaurant's longtime reputation. Afterward, they walked the shoreline's pathway enjoying a close-up view of the marina's boats and, far beyond that, Vancouver's North Shore mountains.

Chapter Ten

On the drive back to Sechelt, Brad decided to surprise Alexis. He said nothing about it until he turned off the highway and approached Porpoise Bay.

She looked at him. “Where are we going?”

“I’m taking you somewhere you’ve never been before.”

“That sounds very interesting. I can see the bay, so we must be close to your house.”

“It’s very close, so close in fact that you can almost see it from here. I’m going to show it to you.”

“How nice,” she enthused. “I wasn’t sure you’d ever let me walk in the door. Like you’re a trap-door spider who only pulls in victims. Am I going to be a victim?”

“I think people are victims only if they want to be. And I’m not sure what a spider’s procedure would be. So we’ll have to call it a no-go.”

They laughed, but if they had really cared to condense what had been said, it might've pointed to interesting possibilities – or none at all.

As he approached his house, he saw a dark car pull out from in front of it and quickly drive away. Mason?

He felt his scalp tighten. A dark blue Ford. Could it be? Giving his head a shake, he parked on his driveway, helped Alexis from the car, and ushered her into the house, saying, “Welcome to my humble abode with no spiders, only me.”

She smiled happily, “What more could one want?”

He took her by the arm and led her into the living room to show her the view of the bay – Porpoise Bay.

Standing there, she touched his arm and said, “It’s beautiful. You have a wonderful location and (gazing behind her) a wonderful home.”

He feigned no notice of her touch. He wondered if Meagan would be so touchy-feely? He doubted it. "Thanks, Alexis. Now, would you like a coffee or a drink of wine? It's well past four."

"Coffee would be nice, thanks."

He went into the kitchen and started the coffee as she stood beside him.

"I can see you've got some lovely things. I like painting sailboats. (pointing) and the art deco figure. Your large refectory-style dinner table looks like Mexican pine. It's lovely. And your glass-fronted barrister bookcase is beautiful."

"It belonged to my parents. I always admired it, and they specifically left it to me in their will. It has a special place in my heart."

She walked over and interestedly looked at book titles. He stood beside her and pointed to a recent thrift-store acquisition. "I found Dostoyevski's book, The Idiot, to be a bit of a hard read. I much preferred his Crime and Punishment."

"I read Crime and Punishment years ago and don't remember much about it. But I do remember enjoying the book," she said. Both of them being book lovers, they launched into a short discussion about favorite books and their authors.

As they sat finishing their coffees, she said, "Your coffee hits the spot and I wish I could stay longer. And," she added with a raised eyebrow, "Maybe next time we'll have it with a shot of our favorite."

He smiled and nodded, "Mexican elixir."

"But tonight Meagan wants me to pop over to her place for dinner and one of her favorite movies. The next time I'm here, I'd like to see the rest of your place."

"Of course. And speaking of Meagan, is she happy with the paint job?"

"She's delighted. There's a bit more to do, but not right away."

He looked at her inquiringly, “Will seemed pretty willing to do it. He’s quite a character. He didn’t appear to be particularly happy with Meagan and me working in the kitchen together. And he became a bit challenging in the way he said he could do a car repair in half the time it took me. He was definitely showing attitude.”

“Well, he can show an attitude, but I find him to be harmless, sort of a man-child with big ideas.”

“But does Meagan want his attention?”

“She definitely doesn’t. In fact, she said he annoys her.”

“Well, when necessary, she should be prepared to tell him to back off.”

“She has, in her own way, which isn’t particularly strong. She’s very soft-hearted and doesn’t want to offend.”

“What’s the story with this guy? Where’s he from, how long has he been here, what does he do?”

Alexis had a sip of coffee and put down her cup. "Apparently, he's from Powell River, up the coast. He rented his place a few months ago. I don't know anything about his personal life, only that he's an electrician. He has seen me at Meagan's place, and one day he saw me at Home Hardware looking at electrical switches. He introduced himself and ended up fixing my lamp that I said wasn't working. Frankly, I find him kind of interesting, and not bad looking, like a painting that's been painted over; there might be something more interesting under the surface." Brad changed the subject.

"So what's Meagan's favorite movie that you're going to see tonight?"

"Grand Hotel, have you seen it? It's on Turner Classics."

"Yes, Greta Garbo and John Barrymore. What a great pair. I read a book about her life, her aversion to publicity and the press. She didn't even show up for some Oscar awards. She had an innate need for solitude and became reclusive. It'd no doubt be exacerbated by her being bipolar, up one moment, depressed the next, never a truly happy person. She was great in the movie."

She smiled. "Now I'm really looking forward to it. Before you take me home, could we go for a quick walk on that pier over there (pointing) and look at the bay?"

They walked to the pier and down its entire length to the end where several dozen boats were moored. There were sailboats and power boats of various sizes and descriptions, all adding up to the lure of the sea and the adventure it promised. She hoped to see it all again.

On the other side of town is the Salish Sea. When in the downtown area, Brad would often walk two blocks to the shoreline where he could feel a unique sense of space and freedom. It had felt especially provocative one stormy day as he watched wind-whipped waves washing ashore. The most popular feature there is Trail Bay Boulevard, a street several blocks long, with a promenade where people can walk by the seaside. A block from the town center, it's a convenient place for locals and visitors alike to stroll anytime.

As he drove Alexis home, she said, "And what do you think of my little sister?"

He thought for a moment. "I think she's quite special the way she interacts with people and does things in such a smooth and easy way. She seems very confident and capable."

"Cute, too, eh?"

He nodded slowly. "She's definitely easy on the eyes. How old is she, if I may ask?"

"Too young for you," she replied, with a twinkle in her eye.

"Wait a minute. How old do you think I am?"

"Oh, I don't know. You're in great shape so it's hard to tell. Forty-five?"

"Close enough. So, really, how old is she?"

"Her birthday is on the sixth of November." (she paused) "Oh, what the heck … she'll be forty and don't tell her I told you."

Brad put up his hand. "It's okay. She already told me she was thirty-nine when she arrived here. I was just testing because many women seem to find it difficult to fess-up their real age. So when is your birthday?"

"Oh I've already mine … March twentieth. And while on the subject, when's yours? He laughed. "I can't remember the last time I was asked … January twenty-third."

"An interesting time of the year. By the way, how much work do you plan on doing at her place? She said you could see things that needed doing."

He scratched his arm. "Some of what I really need to do, the daily-use things, I'll give her a hand with. Beyond that, who knows. Why do you ask?"

"I could see you two getting involved to the point where you're spending a lot of time together. I think you're attracted to her, and she likes you, too. And I, of course, won't be a consideration in any way. I'll be happily living in Mexico. Besides, you treat me as if I'm your sister. I just want to say I appreciate it very much. You don't unnecessarily complicate matters."

He looked at her, thinking about what she said, but left it alone. "In your current mode of transition, the last thing you need is intrigue."

"Thank you, my dear. You're so right."

As he saw her condo coming into view, he said, "By the way, what's Meagan's last name? I never got it when we were introduced."

"It's Atherton, an old English name. If I didn't have a son, I might've changed my married name back to it like Meagan did."

"I didn't know you had a son."

"Oh yes, he's a very talented young man who lives in Palo Alto, California working in the Tesla car company's design area. It's been almost a year since I last saw him. He says he'll visit me in my Mexican home. He also tells me he'll buy me a Tesla car someday." She laughed. "We'll see. In the meantime, we keep in touch."

Arriving at Alexis' condo, Brad again admired the huge southwest panorama taking in the Salish Sea and Vancouver Island. When he parked the car, they sat for a moment gazing at the waterscape. "It's wonderful, isn't it?" she enthused. "You and I both have such nice views."

"I like how yours reaches out into the Salish Sea. I'd have a large telescope on a tripod checking out the cruise ships, (he laughed) and maybe even who's onboard."

She chuckled. "Well, I don't have the same curiosity as you do, but I do have a small, three-power opera glass that lets me see if it's an ocean liner or ferry."

She looked at her watch. "It looks like I've less than an hour to get ready to go to Meagan's. So I'd better get going. She leaned over and gave him a cheek hug. "Thanks for lunch. Let's talk soon."

He drove away thinking about what he had appreciated the first time he met her, she being a strong woman, confident, determined, and aggressive to achieve what she wanted. She was very unlike Meagan who seemed to favor nuances, while giving little away. Before driving home, he picked up a few groceries. As he left the store Will walked in, nodded quickly and carried on, obviously not wanting contact. It left Brad wondering why he'd make it so obvious. It's probably because Meagan doesn't fawn on him like Alexis does. And Meagan and I are friends.

Chapter Eleven

When Brad turned onto his driveway, his cell phone alerted. Minutes later he stood in the kitchen reading a text message from Karen.

"Dear Brad — I have just finished work, and I thought I'd pass along some thoughts. I've been thinking of the irony of my wanting what is considered to be a normal and loving thing, yet it's what drove us apart. I now know we are two different people in so many ways, and our separate aspirations will keep us apart. But I just want you to know that I valued our time spent together. The time was not wasted, and I'll cherish the memories. Love, Karen"

He had looked forward to a quiet evening, but he began to excavate old feelings now overlain with new realities. He set about stripping their relationship down to an essential truth: they had conflicting goals that were only a problem when permanency came into question. Yet there were component issues as well. They were often like ships passing in the night, both busy on selected courses, taking whatever time was necessary. It had increasingly become likely that conflicting thoughts about their future together would eventually set them apart.

He nevertheless appreciated Karen’s sanguine note that no longer placed blame. It sounded heartfelt and sincere and took some gumption to send. He thought about what to say to her.

"Dear Karen – Thanks for your message. I appreciate your honest candor about how we arrived at this point. It’s hard to know what more to say. I want to tell you I've purchased a house in Sechelt quite near the water, which is what I've always wanted. It’s a welcoming community, and I look forward to becoming a productive part of it. My wish for you is a future with abundant health, happiness, and success, and I know you'll achieve it all. Love, Brad"

With his groceries put in the cupboards and fridge, he sat on his recliner and began to relax. His eyes again took in the two larger-than-usual holes in the wall where the previous owner had hung a tapestry. He put aside the urge to get the Pollyfilla and returned a call from Chris. They agreed to get together at the pub Friday night.

That evening, Alexis arrived at Meagan's place with a bottle of Okanagan Sauvignon Blanc wine, one of their favorites.

"Meagan, I have to tell you I ran into Will at the liquor store a while ago. We had a brief chat, and he managed to wheedle it out of me that I was going to your place this evening. You won't believe this, but he said he might drop by. But before I could say it wasn't a good idea, he left the store."

Meagan looked aghast. "That's the last thing I want. This is supposed to be our night. I don't want him showing up here. He always wants to be a good boy scout and be helpful, but he only wants to spend time with us. In fact, his self-important and arrogant attitude makes me feel uncomfortable, like having a big spider in the room. I shouldn't have let him help us paint; it only encouraged him. And I think there's another side to him that we saw when he took delight in shooting Brad down with his supposed better repair expertise. He wants to look more handy. Plus, I think he's jealous of Brad, especially his helping me in the kitchen. If he comes here tonight, I'll tell him this is our night, and you can back me up."

"You should also tell him it's polite to visit only if invited, saying it, of course, in a friendly yet firm way like you mean it."

As if in a queue, there was a knock on the door. The women looked at each other, startled – it couldn't be! Meagan went to the door, opened it, her mouth dropping as Will stepped forward.

"Hi Meagan, hi Alexis. I was driving by on my way home when I thought I'd stop and pour you ladies a drink of Jamaican rum before your movie."

He had obviously been drinking, and he now imposed himself heedless of just how insensitive his actions were.

Meagan stood in front of him, barring further entrance. “Alexis and I are having a girl’s night, and I’d appreciate it if you'd let us have our evening without interruption. And we don’t want your rum, thank you very much. We’re having wine.”

“So you don’t want me to even have a short visit? You girls can drink your wine while I have a drink of rum.”

“Will, listen to me,” she said, now freely showing her annoyance. “We don’t want other company tonight. It’s a girl’s night with girl talk and all that. So you’ll have to have your rum at home… okay?”

“You’ve probably got mister smoothie coming by, is that it?” Will taunted. “I’ll be really pissed off if I see his car here tonight, and who would blame me?”

She looked at Will piercingly. “Okay, Will, no one else is coming tonight, so please go.”

Alexis stood firmly beside her, with an arm

around her waist, proud of her sister's determined demeanor.

"Or what are you going to do, beat me up?" He laughed as he stepped out the door.

She could only shake her head slowly. "Can you believe it? I suspected there's something nasty in his makeup, hidden behind his mask of helpfulness. Now I've seen it."

Alexis dropped her arm from Meagan's waist and sat down. "I think it's mostly because he's had quite a bit to drink tonight. After that bit of drama, I could use one, too." Meagan went to the kitchen, poured two glasses of wine, and set them on her coffee table. As they sat sipping their wine Meagan said, "Sometimes the men who want to be nice and helpful are the ones most bent out of shape. They were spoiled when young and haven't grown up with mature thought processes. They're used to having things their way and still think they're special. When Will realized he wasn't going to have things his way about things, he became resentful and accusing." "Because you were infertile?" Alexis said.

"The whole story is we didn't seriously want to have children until several years after we were married. Then my chromosomal type of infertility was diagnosed, and that's when he went off the rails, saying we had waited to have children and now this. And he wouldn't adopt a child. It had to be his own offspring. Then I heard that he and a woman at his office were having an affair, obviously the reason he often came home late at night – 'important meeting.' That's when——" "Your husband was a self-centered idiot," Alexis interjected.

"That's when I began developing an exit plan. I slept in the guest bedroom while Adam fumed and threatened. Then one night he tried to enter the bedroom, but I had the door blocked by a chair." "What the hell do you think you're doing?" he shouted.

"I told him I wanted to stay away from him

because as far as I was concerned we we're through. That's when he started calling me names: a quitter, not a real woman, a partial woman. The next day I put the rest of my plan in motion, phoning my friend Gail to say everything was set. I'd move in with my personal items that day. Then I left a note for Adam who was at work. I told him I was going to stay with Gail until I got my own place. So I settled in with her, and several days later I hired a lawyer and began divorce proceedings."

Alexis nodded approvingly. "And what did Gail have to say about it?"

"She said she's seen worse. And now that I had seen a worse side of Adam, I didn't know how much worse it could get."

Alexis shook her head. "I've heard of men being concerned solely about them being dumped. It didn't fit their picture of their worthiness, their manliness, and they'll get her back no matter what it takes. Men like that can indeed become dangerous."

Meagan put up her hand. “I read up on the subject and saw nothing surprising. They will sometimes spy on the woman to know what she’s doing and if she’s seeing another man. I knew the best thing was not to give him a chance to meet for discussions, make it clear it’s over-with.”

“When was the last time you heard from him?”

“It’s been about a year. Plus, we’re now divorced. I’m so glad it’s over. It’s such a worrisome waste of time and energy. I’ll bet Brad wouldn’t be like that.”

“Well, I think that’s a safe bet,” Alexis said, knowingly. “You like him and I do, too. He’s intelligent, considerate, and fun to be around. We had a good time today shopping at The Brick. He bought a washer and dryer, and we had lunch at Molly's Reach Restaurant. When we came back, he showed me his house.”

“How nice,” Meagan said lightly. “Maybe someday I can see it, too.”

Then, seeing a look of impatience on Alexis' face, she changed the subject. “By the way, I've been meaning to ask you about something you said regarding Will being at your place a while ago to do some repairs. What kind of repairs?”

“I told him about my lamp not working. He insisted on fixing it. So he did, and I made lunch. He acts like he knows me because he sees me coming and going at your place. He’s easy to have around even though he’s not much of a conversationalist … a bit narrow in that category. But all in all, I find him to be a reasonably attractive man-child from whom I expect nothing exceptional.”

“Do you find him sexually attractive? Would you invite him over for the night?”

Alexis laughed. “What a question. I really hadn’t thought about it. Not seriously, at least. And how about you and Brad, can you see a hot relationship developing?”

Meagan thought for a moment. “I don’t know if

I'm ready for a hot relationship after what Adam put me through. But, yes, I'd like to get to know him better. He seems quite special."

Alexis nodded. "He's a decent kind of guy who has shown he has a good heart. I can see you two getting together, and who knows the outcome? It is said that as with grief and happiness, you never know when to expect love."

Meagan looked surprised and smiled. "Even so, I could understand it if before you go to Mexico you and Will have some sort of dalliance. Something of the moment and then … zip … you're gone."

Alexis laughed. "Though I might consider Will a boy toy, I could really fall for Brad, but he's too much man for me to trifle with."

Meagan thought for a moment and quickly said, "Let's have another glass."

At the pub Friday evening, Brad and Chris, as usual, talked about hiking, the upcoming hockey season, and like all men, they talked about women, in the present, the past, and the foreseeable future.

“So, Chris, how long were you married?”

“I married at thirty-six; my wife Carolyn was twenty-nine. After five years, we divorced last year. We had no children because neither of us really wanted children. At least one of us should have been more domestically dynamic.”

“Strange how things work out. The differences between Karen and me are what ended it. She wanted children, I didn’t. I already have a grown son and daughter. I’m forty-nine, and Karen’s at an age when many single women begin to think about their waning child-bearing years. My thinking about early retirement added to the improbability of starting child rearing. There’s no way I wanted to start a family again. In fact, I’m perfectly comfortable spending a good amount of alone time. What Wordsworth describes as the joy of solitude.”

“I’m happy in my own skin, too. But you know

as I do that it's nice to have a woman in your life to round it out and have the comforts that come with it, even if she's just a friend, at least some kind of relationship. It's been a year, and I've only recently recovered from the loss and loneliness of divorce."

"Haven't you met a woman since you've been single that you could start a relationship with?"

Chris put down his glass. "It's not easy to find a good match. For instance, Sechelt has one of the province's largest populations of seniors, as I'm sure you've noticed. I've had drinks with a couple of women in the hiking group, but nothing's come of it. As I get older and they get older, we become more… what's the word?"

"Sidelined, jaded?" Brad laughed.

"I'm not sure, but what's missing are truly romantic feelings that get things started, the fuel for the fire. I'm a romantic, maybe an incurable romantic. And in the past year, I haven't met a woman who exudes any romanticism or sex appeal. What I mainly look for, at least in the beginning, is a woman with intelligence, cordiality, and good humor. Good looks and sex appeal are icing on the cake."

As Chris described the woman he'd be attracted to, Brad's mind went to Meagan. She was that kind of woman, the kind of woman he wanted to get to know better.

Chris picked up his glass and said, "Have you met anyone since coming here?"

"I have. Her name's Meagan, sweet person, attractive and intelligent. The funny thing is that I met her sister first."

As they finished their dinner, Brad went on to tell how he met Alexis and how she introduced him to Meagan. He told about her house, the work done, and how much more he wanted to help her.

Chris smiled. "Sounds to me like you've already got some pretty strong feelings for the woman."

Brad looked at his empty glass and nodded. “Yeah, I do.”

“I can tell. Consider yourself lucky.”

They paid their dinner bills, and as they walked to their cars, Chris said, “I’ll send you an email with information about next Monday’s hike. It’ll be a good one.”

Brad waved. “Looking forward to it.”

Chapter Twelve

Brad always savored his Saturday morning coffee, a time to relax and think about what to do for the rest of the day. On such a morning, a glance over the coffee cup rim centered once again on those two nail holes in the wall. Unlike other times, there was no excuse to do nothing about them. He finished his coffee, got his Pollyfilla, and carefully filled the holes, keeping within their circumferences and smoothing them carefully.

Hours later, with the Pollyfilla fully set, he got out the small can of paint the owner had left for touch-ups. When the spots were painted and had dried, they perfectly matched the rest of the wall. Good job, he thought. He had also been meaning to phone Eric and Connie and, finding their number in the phone book, he made the call.

Connie answered. “Hi Brad, it’s nice to hear from you. I’m sorry you just missed Eric. He went downtown and won’t be back until lunchtime. He’ll call you back. You'll have to come and visit us soon."

"Hi Connie, I'll look forward to his call, and we can set something up."

After saying their goodbyes, he began his plan for the day. In the afternoon, he bought the parts needed for Meagan's fix-ups. At Home Hardware, he bought twenty-eight adjustable hinges and the O-ring. He next went to The Brew House. Adel not only prepared an excellent espresso, but she also made him feel welcome, like he was a long-time customer. The shop had become one of his favorite stops, mostly for her flavorful coffee. The first time he went there, he asked for a regular coffee with a shot of espresso, what she called a shot in the dark. This time, wanting to try something stronger, he asked for a long double espresso. She smiled and handed it to him, saying, "Here you are, a long-pull double espresso."

"Is that what it's called?"

"A long double espresso is good, too," she

replied, with a warm smile.

As usual, when he left the shop, he felt uplifted and inspired by Adel's bonhomie. And she was so easy to look at. While walking to his car, he felt the next part of his agenda should be a long walk. He drove to Kinnikinnick Park and hiked the orange trail twice, a total of six kilometers. It felt perfect. Much of his fitness behavior began in his school days where his competitive athletic side showed itself; he reveled in fitness challenges. In his adult life, he had certifications in karate and scuba diving, and involvement in things from hockey and football to hiking. By the time he turned fifty, he had only minor injuries to show for his sporting involvements – little to complain about.

Later that day, Eric phoned. His goodwill and friendliness were exactly what Brad needed. He wasn't yet well socialized. Eric invited him to dinner the following week. He suggested Wednesday at five o'clock and said Brad needn't bring anything to drink

– he had ouzo, wine, and beer. The invitation came as a surprise, and it warmed Brad to know he'd again be spending time with them. He next phoned Meagan to set up a time to install the parts he bought. She took his call while in the middle of making dinner. He didn't tie her up with extraneous conversation, and they agreed to meet at one o'clock Sunday, her day off.

After speaking with him, Meagan continued washing vegetables, thinking about his friendly and easy way of communicating, a big change from her husband Adam. He either talked too much or, in the final year of their marriage, sometimes not much at all. Now, being truly freed from a hurtful past, her only thoughts of it were things that reminded her of the differences – such as Brad. He was a special kind of man she never expected to meet, especially in a small town. But, she thought (smiling) miracles could happen, and looked forward to getting to know him better.

When she met Brad, she saw a man with an

open and positive attitude. The first time he talked to her, she could hear who he was, a man not only intelligent but also sensible and caring. And he didn't zigzag and play games like some other men she met. He came across as a genuine article, helpful and easy to be around, and with a great sense of humor. His good looks were easy on the eyes, too.

Seeing him and being around him aroused something in her she hadn't felt in a long time. She loved the sound of his voice, a smooth baritone. She had to admit to herself that even on the phone with him she sometimes felt aroused. The trouble was that she didn't have the confidence to do something about it. Adam had demeaned it out of her. She had nevertheless begun telling herself to begin trying. Forget Adam's words. Now was the time to do it.

Since the day they met, Brad's feelings for Meagan had become increasingly awakened. He felt enlivened by her graciousness, warmth, and personality, her wholesomeness and beauty. She was like a jewel found in an environment that doesn't promise treasure. The kitchen fix-ups would be an opportunity to get to know her better. I won't be flattering, something she'd no doubt be accustomed to hearing, he thought. He'd instead maintain a sensible amount of sangfroid.

On Sunday, he drove to Meagan's house keeping an eye out for Mason. His release could be anytime soon and, if he showed up in Sechelt, Brad wanted to meet him head-on. No surprises. As he approached Meagan's door she opened. "Hi Brad, one o'clock, you're right on time. Would you like a coffee before you start?"

He stood with his toolbox in his hand and a smile on his face. "That sounds great, but how about if I do some work first? Coffee in say an hour or so?"

"Alright, at two or two-thirty," she said. "And while you're being productive I'll paint some trim. Call it an inspired project. You're a good influence. Not that I'm lazy, but one can get so used to seeing needy things that they almost disappear."

"No kidding. I had a couple of large nail holes in my wall that I finally got around to filling and painting yesterday. By the way, how was your girl's movie night? Did you enjoy the movie?"

"Well, the evening had an added performance. I don't want to get into it right now. Let's talk about it when we have coffee. Give me a shout if you need anything."

He unpacked the O-ring and hinges, wondering what the added performance could possibly be. Could it be something she and/or Alexis did or said? Were there things they had to settle, or did someone else enter into it? If someone else, who? With these thoughts in his mind, he walked to the kitchen sink, turned off the water, took the faucet apart, and replaced the O'Ring. With the water turned on, the faucet was drip-free. Then he began replacing old hinges with the new, adjustable ones. By the time Meagan returned to the kitchen a little more than an hour later, most of the new hinges on the bottom doors had been installed.

“Wow, that’s fast work. Ready for coffee?”

“Sounds good.”

Now feeling the closeness of the two of them together in the small kitchen, he felt the same warm body flash and quickening of the heart that took him by surprise the last time. For Meagan, the same feelings were becoming more intense than she had ever felt before with any man, including her husband. She thought, as she often did, Why the hell did I marry him? Brad once again helped her reach for the cups. As he stood beside her, he became infused with her aura and fragrance, a bouquet of femininity.

She suddenly turned to him. “I want to pay you for the parts. Did you bring the receipt?”

“I did,” he said, reaching into his pocket and handing it to her. She went to her bedroom, came back with money, and sweetly said, “Keep the change" – it being seventy-five cents.

He chuckled, "Thanks, big spender."

Meagan smiled and poured two cups of coffee. "Go ahead and add what you want, then we can relax in the living room."

As they sat on the sofa, she told how Will had shown up. "He simply knocked on the door and walked in as if he had been invited. Alexis and I were both shocked, especially when we realized by his composure and way of talking that he had been drinking quite a lot."

"Was he in any way threatening?"

"No. He said he wanted to pour us a drink of rum and couldn't understand why we refused it. When I asked him to leave, he got quite snooty and asked if you were coming. I think he sees you as the reason I don't want him around. I don't want him around at all," she emphasized.

Brad put down his coffee cup and looked at her.

"You shouldn't have to guard against a guy who hasn't the common sense to be polite and know when he is or isn't wanted. I actually wondered why he'd be here painting."

"He's a really busybody and often goes by on his walks to who knows where. When he saw me get out of my car with pails of paint, he stopped and asked me what I was going to paint. When I told him, he said he had done a lot of house painting for a construction company he once worked for and said he'd be glad to help. So like a fool, I agreed he could help Alexis and me do it. She likes him a lot. She even encourages it sometimes with the things she says. And, as you know, she has let him be her on-call repairman. She likes him, thinks he's cute. Never mind the fact he can be quite out of tune."

Brad snickered. "Well, I know he has an attitude. I saw it when I met him on painting day. He acted like a herd bull defying the competition, definitely not friendly. I saw it again the other day in

Clayton's Market. He hardly acknowledged me."

Meagan shook her head. "That's too bad. But come to think of it, I've been made to think of him when I've heard unusual sounds around the outside of the house late at night."

"What kinds of sounds?"

"I'm not sure. Sometimes it's so vague, I think I might be imagining it. Then at other times, there's a slight tap or scraping sound along the wall … maybe not scraping, more like something brushing against the wall."

"So what do you think it could be?"

"I don't know, maybe raccoons. I'm told they apparently like to dig around houses looking for insects and mice. Someone said even deer will lurk around houses at night if they smell certain kinds of vegetation."

"Has it ever frightened you?"

"Yes, I thought there could be someone lurking

outside my bedroom window. One night I even huddled under my blanket like a child afraid of a bogeyman."

"You shouldn't have to put up with something that is upsetting. Keep track of the sounds and when they happen. As a matter of fact, when you hear them, phone me, quietly of course, and I'll be here in five minutes to check it out. Even so, I don't think you're in any danger at all."

"Thanks, Brad. I really appreciate your concern and willingness to help."

"The main thing is don't let things worry you. Security is close at hand," he said with a grin. "Now I've got more doors to finish. I can keep working, but I don't want it to get into your dinner time, so I'd better get at it."

She raised her hand. "Why not make it our dinner time? How much longer will you be?"

"A couple of hours should do it."

“You keep going, and when you finish, we’ll have a drink and relax … unless you have other plans tonight, of course.”

He shook his head. “I've nothing planned, and thanks.”

As he walked to the kitchen, he turned. “By the way, how long have you been hearing these sounds?”

“Oh, about a month or so.”

As he installed the hinges and realigned the doors, he thought about what Meagan had told him. It wasn't that damned Mason. He hasn’t been released yet.

When all the cupboard doors had been hinged and adjusted, the couple had their drinks and conversed as though they had known each other for years. They later sat down to a dinner that happened to be one of his favorites – beef stew. He complimented her, saying it had been one of the best he'd enjoyed.

He said, "My mother used to make a lot of beef stews. It was my dad's favorite, and mine too. Yours is in the same delicious category."

Later, when he was about to leave, she stood in the kitchen opening and closing some of the cupboard doors.

"The doors open and close so nicely," she enthused. "I can't thank you enough. I should have also paid you for your work."

"You could cover that with something as simple as another stew. Call it quid pro quo."

"We can definitely do that," she said as they walked to the door.

There they stood, each feeling the heady drug of attraction and the disquiet of heightened emotions. Unlike Alexis, who would have enjoyed a hug and a kiss, Brad's feelings in the matter were stalled by Meagan's inscrutable persona that spoke of patience

– a definite case of je ne sais quoi. As he drove away, he replayed the fact that he hadn't done anything that would suggest he didn't respect the nuances of getting to know this beguiling woman. He had been warm and friendly, not foolishly aggressive.

In fact, both had played their hands well, and both were falling in love, adding yet more fuel to whatever fate had in store for them.

Chapter Thirteen

When at Eric and Connie's house for dinner on Wednesday, Brad was quickly reminded of the comfort he felt in being with good friends.

"Welcome, Brad," Eric said. "We were looking forward to seeing you. It seems like a long time since you were last here."

"Glad to be here," he happily chipped in.

In the living room, he again sat on the exquisitely made wooden chair with its intricately embroidered seat. He ran his hand over the finely shaped and highly polished arms. "I was impressed with this chair the last time I sat in it. You said you made it?"

Eric turned and pointed. "Right there in the shop by the house. I make furniture, actually anything made of wood."

"Well, I see a lot of nice things when I go into furniture stores," Brad said, "but I don't recall seeing anything as stylish as this chair. Not only the style, but the wood as well. What kind is it?"

"It's Brazilian Tiger Mahogany. I like it because it has a good variety of grain colors and patterns, and it's a very hard wood. It takes more work than most others, but it's worth it."

Brad stroked the wood again. "Absolutely, if it ends up looking like this."

He looked at Connie, "And the embroidery compliments it so well."

"A small contribution compared to what he put into it," she said. "He can sometimes work up a pretty good sweat trying to get the wood to cooperate. I'm sometimes tempted to hose him down."

Eric chuckled. "True enough. Especially on a really warm day. So Brad, we have beer, wine, and the Greek prince of drinks, ouzo. What'll you have?"

"Ouzo sounds good, with a bit of water, please."

“Connie, you’ll have the same?”

“Yes, dear.”

As they relaxed, the conversation focused on Brad’s previous life and work in Vancouver, and quickly turned to his being in Sechelt. He told how he came to be there, how he was tired of big-city business and the pace of life. He outlined what he liked about living on the Sunshine Coast – the natural environment, walking and hiking in it, the slowed-down pace – and how he planned on staying in it. Eric said they’d lived in Sechelt for sixteen years, coming from Toronto where he worked for a furniture manufacturer. Like Brad, he wanted a change, a new start. His customer base now mainly consists of specialty-furniture stores and appreciative individuals. Connie had worked at the Urban Mode furniture store, where they met.

As dinnertime approached, Eric took charge of preparing barbecued sirloin steaks and baked potatoes. The meal included Connie’s sumptuous shrimp salad, with home-made baklava for dessert. Dinner was enjoyed with lively discussions covering a range of topics, much of it about Brad's plans and expectations. After dinner, Eric asked him if he'd like another drink.

Connie stood up and walked to the kitchen. "Or tea or coffee?" Both men settled on tea.

"That's three teas. Be right back." As Connie left the room, she turned to Eric. "I've fed Plato, so he'll be civilized if I let him in."

"Sounds good," he replied, and turning to Brad said, "You'll like him."

"You've really got my curiosity now. Who's Plato?"

"He's our good buddy out on the back porch; he's been very polite while we had dinner. He's sure to be happy to see you. He's not rambunctious, so we don't have to worry about him being a nuisance. Here he comes."

A large Black Labrador Retriever, his tail wagging, went straight to Eric.

“This is Plato. He’s been with us for eight years. He’s well trained and is a perfect gentleman … well almost perfect.”

“I haven’t been up close to a Lab since a friend had one years ago,” Brad said as he studied the dog. “It looked exactly like Plato. He sure loved that dog. He named it Major.”

“We love Plato, too, and he loves us, don’t you?” he said, looking at the smiling dog.

Connie came back and sat down. “The tea will be ready in a few minutes. Come here, Plato.”

The dog walked to her, and she stroked his head lovingly.

“Go say hi to Brad.” she said, pointing. Plato calmly walked over, sniffed his knee, and got a pat on his head.

“Plato’s an important part of our family,” Eric said.

Brad nodded. “I think my friend Dave felt the same way about his dog. But he ended up giving him away. I should say reluctantly and sadly gave him away.”

Eric looked startled. “Why would he do that?”

Brad sat back. “When Major was five months old, Dave took him along when he visited a friend’s farm. His friend’s dog and Major soon went on a romp together and Major never came back.”

Connie hurried to the kitchen. “If you’re telling a dog story, wait until I get back with tea.” She returned minutes later, and Brad continued.

“When Dave lost Major, he was devastated. He drove everywhere looking for him and asked people around town if they had seen him. He later contacted the newspaper and began placing a lost-dog ad with Major’s photo. Several weeks later, a woman from a neighboring town phoned to say she saw the ad, and it might be his dog she had found wandering beside the highway. He limped badly with what turned out to be a fractured leg, probably from being hit by a car. She said she took the dog to a vet who set the leg and put it in a cast."

"At least she had the sense to get the leg looked after," Eric interjected.

Brad nodded. "Dave asked the woman if he could see if it was his dog. She somewhat hesitantly agreed and they made an appointment for him to go to her house the following day. On the phone, she had stressed how much her six-year-old daughter loved the dog. She said her husband had died the previous year and the dog had made the girl's life so much happier."

Eric winced. "Ouch, that sounds like a hint – don't come."

"Dave said he felt nervous going to the woman's house, not knowing if it'd be difficult to get Major back."

Eric snorted. "I'd damn well get him."

Brad continued. “At the house the next day, the woman ushered Dave into her living room where the little girl, Lisa, sat on the sofa holding onto Major’s collar. She called him Max. But get this, the dog showed little if any recognition of Dave. Needless to say, he was shocked and disappointed. A vet friend of his later told him it isn’t a surprising result when a young dog with a traumatic injury is fawned over for a period of time by people like the little girl and her mother. Dave showed his photo of Major, pointing out his white-spot chest markings that were the same as the dog Lisa held.”

Connie looked aghast. “So there was no doubt that the dog was Major, did the mother not see it?”

“She did, but the little girl said some dogs must have the same markings, and she began to cry as she held onto the dog’s collar. When the mother told her the dog really did belong to Dave, the little girl sobbed ‘no … mommy … no …’ Dave said he began to feel like an intruder. And the mother began getting teary-eyed seeing her daughter's tears. Anyhow, the mother took hold of the collar and made the little girl let go."

Connie shook her head. "That must have been tough."

"The girl went screaming no, no to her bedroom, with the dog trying to follow her. The mother held the dog's collar and gave Dave its leash. The woman, he said, looked distraught. He thought she'd break into tears at any moment. When he left the room he began almost pulling Major to the car. He said he felt as if he was stealing a dog that not only didn't know him but didn't even seem to belong to him. In the car the poor thing stood confused. Dave lifted it in."

When the car started, the dog began whimpering. Dave patted its head and talked to him, but the dog didn't seem to hear him, it heard something else. Then Dave heard it, too. He turned and saw Lisa running from the house wailing,

'Maaax, Maaax'. Then she dropped to the sidewalk on her knees, sobbing pitifully with outstretched hands, crying 'nooo, nooo, Maax, noooo.'"

Connie put her hand to her face. "You're going to make me cry."

Brad said, "Dave sat there stunned by the little girl's emotional appeal. It put him in a turmoil wondering what was the right thing to do. He could see that the dog had become as much Lisa's as his – her love and care – and then the loss of her father and the happiness Major brought to her. The only conclusion he could come to was that she needed the dog as much or even more than he did."

Eric leaned forward. "Don't keep us in suspense."

"To Dave there seemed to be only one thing he could do to solve the situation with a clear conscience."

Eric leaned further. "And?"

"He simply opened the car door and watched Major bound out into the little girl's arms. He said he walked back and saw the happiest little girl and dog he'd ever expect to see again. He said he knew he'd done the right thing when he saw the girl's joy. Her mother was in tears and shaking her head in disbelief and happiness. He said at that point he couldn't help being a bit teary-eyed himself."

"Wow, I could never give Plato away like that," Eric said.

"He'd rather give me away," Connie quipped. "Eric, you might do it, too, if the dog no longer knew you. But the difference here is that Plato's been with us for eight years. He'd always know us even if we were away for a few months a year, or more."

Eric nodded in thought. "Still, quite a story, makes me appreciate having him even more."

"Yes, he's our boy," said Connie, looking fondly at the dog. "And now, Brad, can I get you some more baklava?"

"No thanks, Connie. I'm full up and happy to relax and chat. I really don't know much about you and Eric yet. One thing I'm curious about, do you have children?"

Eric slowly nodded, "We had a daughter who died in a boating accident years ago on Lake Ontario."

"She was only twenty… a beautiful girl," Connie said, and looked at Eric as if for emotional support.

"Well, it shouldn't have happened," Eric said emphatically. "The boat driver had little experience. One evening at high tide and when it was almost dark, he drove under a low pier and crashed. They both died."

With sincere feelings, Brad said he was sorry and had heard of it happening before.

Connie said, "What about you, Brad? Do you have children?"

"Yes, a daughter. She lives in Vancouver.

She's like me, single, and we visit back and forth."

"Don't you have a serious other?"

Brad smiled accommodatingly. "I did have, but after three years together, our different expectations put a kibosh on it. She was thirty-seven, wanted to get married and start a family. At this stage of my life, I didn't want to start another family. Other than that, we had a good relationship and could have remained together. So we finally tried a one-month trial separation to see if either of us would change our mind and I ended up coming here alone. End of story."

Eric nodded, sat lost in thought for a moment, and looked at Brad. "Would you like another ouzo? I'll join you if you do."

"I normally would, but I'm a bit tired tonight. And I don't like to drive even if I've had only two drinks unless I'm staying the night."

Connie smiled. "We have a guest bedroom

should it ever be needed."

"There could be a day when we have more than two drinks you know," Eric said. "There's such a thing as the Greek mid-February Carnival Season. It's similar to Mardi Gras in New Orleans. We invite a few of our local Greek friends over and watch some of the events taking place in Greece. My parents were born in Skyros. I'm a first-generation Canadian. Connie's something like fifth."

"Oh, poo, I'm third generation. How about you Brad?"

"I'm third generation. In the late eighteen hundreds, my great-grandfather was a Nova Scotia merchant seaman who used to buy and sell goods up and down the Atlantic coast all the way down to Argentina."

"That's a coincidence," Eric said. "My ancestors were sea goers, too. Shipping and fishing. Skyros is an island, so it's a usual kind of business."

“I think I've inherited the seagoing urge,” Brad said. “I love being on the water. And near it, too. I thought about buying a boat in Vancouver, but decided not to get weighed down with more things. Now, being here makes me realize having a boat wouldn’t be such a bad idea.”

“I think it's easier to rent a boat sometime,” Eric suggested.

“Remind me to buy a life vest,” said Connie.

Eric lowered his brow. “My dear, you can float perfectly well. I've seen you many times.”

“You can float a heck of a lot higher than I can.”

He laughed. “Sometime we’ll have to talk more about our ancestors and boats. I’ll show you some photos.”

For Brad, the evening had been replete, with an excellent dinner and the company of a couple who were husband and wife, and friends, too. They liked to touch on a broad range of subjects, sometimes competitively, but not truly so. Being with them was like being with close family. He drove home looking forward to the next time. As he drove, he checked his rearview mirror and saw nothing unusual – not yet.

Chapter Fourteen

Brad arrived home shortly after ten o'clock, and while standing in the kitchen pouring a glass of water, his phone rang. He answered it to hear Alexis' happy voice. "There you are. I didn't think you'd be out this late."

"Hi Alexis. What's happening?"

"Oh, not much. I just wanted to have a quick chat with you and tell you I've taken the final step to securing my Mexican house. I sent the papers and a cheque yesterday, and I'm hoping construction will commence before or soon after Christmas."

"That's good news. Nothing to worry about now."

"I had planned on Meagan going there with me for Christmas, but she now tells me she isn't sure about it, with her new work responsibilities and other things. I'm not quite sure what the other things are."

"I couldn't say. She likes to be busy," he said,

not wanting to expand on it.

"It'd be wonderful if you'd both be there with me," she enthused. "It'd be fun."

"I don't think I could really justify going; this time of year it'd be best to attend to things here."

"What kind of things? You and Meagan seem terribly involved in things. She laughed. "I'm just kidding. We should all be as lucky as you two."

He could tell Alexis had been drinking, and knew it could be a waste of time discussing relationship issues. So he took another route.

"You probably told me before, but what are you going to do with all of your furniture?"

She gave him the full report on the matter, the gist of being that she'd sell most of it. She then apologized for phoning so late.

"I'm not usually up until this hour. Frankly, I'm quite tired of going to bed early. There must be more for single people my age to do at night."

"Well," said Brad. "Sechelt has an older demographic and that's to be somewhat expected. You'll find that —"

"But I'll be moving soon and I can guarantee you that there is a more dynamic nightlife at Lake Chapala."

They ended their conversation with plans to get together soon if only for coffee.

Brad had felt Alexis' interest in him on many occasions, sometimes more subtle than others. She liked touching, and with each touch came a message: "Look at me, do you like what you see." Meagan, on the other hand, had the kind of mind and personality he could relate to best. His emerging feelings for her screamed at him: find out more about her and what she expects in life. After all, it could all end up being nothing more than something hoped for.

Monday's hike took in eight kilometers at Cliff Gilker Park. Brad and Chris walked awhile together chatting as usual. Another hiker walked near them and threw in a few comments about the trail and the beautiful scenery; others were strung out in a line, each in his or her own natural world of enjoyment. The trail eventually led down a slope to a stone-covered beach on the shore of the Salish Sea.

"This is one of my favorite hikes," Chris said. "Very often we see seals staring back at us. Then there's the perpetual gulls and other shore birds. One time we even saw a just-born seal pup left on the beach while its mother went off no doubt in search of food. The pup looked okay and we could see it breathing. It laid quietly with its eyes closed. Someone suggested we take it to Gibsons Wildlife Rehabilitation Centre, but after some discussion, we voted it down and carried on, certain that the mother would return."

"It's a beautiful shoreline," Brad enthused. "I love being near the ocean and seeing its expanse all the way to the horizon. I also enjoy looking out my window and seeing the bay, mountains, eagles soaring, the planes and boats coming and going. It's interesting to simply see the varying textures of the water. By the way, where do you live?"

"I have a condo on Trail Avenue near the senior's center. It's close to everything, I can walk anywhere downtown in minutes. You'll have to drop by for a drink sometime. I'll remind you."

After slipping and sliding on the rocks for a couple of kilometers, the group went back on the trail that wound through the magnificent rainforest to the parking lot. Walking beneath the high canopy, and feeling the quiet spirituality of the trees, further validated Brad's choice of this special coast.

After the hike, he hurried home to do what he had on his mind all day.

At well past six o'clock he phoned Meagan. Receiving no answer, he left a message saying he'd be home all evening. Later, as he placed the dinner dishes in the dishwasher, she called.

Meagan sounded urgent and out of breath. “Thank goodness you’re there. I just had the most scary time with Will.”

“What happened?”

“I had just arrived home from work and heard a knock on my door. When I opened the door, Will stood there with a stupid grin on his face. He said he came by to apologize for crashing my movie night with Alexis. I thanked him for his apology, and he walked toward me. When I backed up, he walked into the house. He seemed determined to be with me.”

“Meagan, with guys like him you have to show firmness. Anything less than that is what they rely on to get what they want.”

“I know, but he did it so quickly, like a well-practiced tactic.”

“So what did you do?”

“I was taken aback for a moment, and then I said I was expecting you to drop by and he should leave now. Then with a leer, he said, 'Okay, see ya.'"

"Wow, that's pretty bad behavior to throw at you like that. Did you feel threatened?"

"Not really, but if he'd refused to leave or tried to move closer to me I would have. He seems to think he's above reproach, as if he's god's gift to women. Anyhow, I was so glad to see you'd called."

"I called because I want to invite you to dinner at my place on Saturday. After the delicious meal I enjoyed at your place, I'd like to put on my chef's hat and reciprocate."

"That sounds wonderful. I have to work until six, but I could aim for six-thirty. Would that be alright?"

"That would be great! I'm thinking about having sockeye salmon with rice and a Greek salad. What would you enjoy for dessert?"

"Your dinner sounds delicious, and dessert is your choice. It's been a long time since anyone cooked dinner for me. I'll look forward to it."

"Well, I know it's past your dinner time, Meagan, so I won't keep you. And I'll look forward to seeing you on Saturday."

"See you then. Thank you, Brad."

"Are you going to be alright tonight?"

"Yes, thanks. I'll be fine."

After they said goodbye, Brad did a clumsy imitation of a pirouette for doing what he had been wanting to do since waking. He could now ardently look forward to enjoying an evening with Meagan in his home, something unimaginable only weeks ago. He'd have liked to see her before next Saturday, but she had a full-time job and he needed some time to prepare for their evening together.

Days later, while reading The Coast Journal, the town's weekly newspaper, Brad saw its ad seeking a writer, and he felt a first flash of inspiration. Getting back to media writing and the dignity of work is what he had intended to do in semi-retirement.

With a rush of anticipation, he quickly dashed off an email to the editor with some writing samples.

On Saturday he shopped for things he needed for his dinner. His first stop was the local supermarket for an assortment of items, beginning with things needed for a Greek salad: cucumber, tomato, onion, red pepper, feta cheese, and pitted Kalamata olives. For dessert, he looked in the store's bakery showcase for something with chocolate. Meagan really liked chocolate. He did, too. Seeing nothing that stood out to him, he looked in the frozen-dessert freezer and picked a sure winner: chocolate cheesecake. He next went to the Sechelt Fish Market for sockeye salmon filets, and then the liquor store for a bottle of Sauvignon Blanc, a wine Meagan enjoyed.

By the time he got home, he had begun to wind himself into production mode. But first, because he had plenty of time, he'd go for a walk around Sechelt Marsh, only a few blocks from his home. He enjoyed seeing populations of ducks and other birds. Great blue Herons were often seen wading in the shallows, their long beaks snapping up fish fingerlings. As usual, people were feeding the birds, watched over by the ever-ravenous crows, pigeons, and gulls.

He wanted to enjoy a leisurely walk and have time to think about what he had heard about Leonard Mason. A day earlier, his friend Jeffery called to say that Mason had achieved statutory release and parole. Even though released, he'd be subject to strict rules relating to his comings and goings. Brad would take no chances with Mason on the loose. He felt obligated, both for himself and Meagan, to keep up on Mason's whereabouts. Now I've really got to be on my toes.

He did four laps around the marsh before heading home, leaving a couple of hours to get dinner ready and have a shower before Meagan arrived. She being a highly anticipated guest, he had planned the evening accordingly. He paid special attention to such things as the music and the layout of the table that would see them sitting across from each other. The table being so large, sitting at each end of it would look formal and even laughable.

As he showered and dressed, he envisioned her sitting with him at the table, beautiful and radiating her special aura. He thought again about how when first meeting her at her house on painting day, he never dreamed this day would happen. Later, as he walked to the kitchen to prepare the Greek salad, Chris phoned.

"Hey Brad, I wasn't sure if I'd find you home on a nice day like this."

"Hi Chris. I just did four laps around the marsh. I can't simply do nothing on such a perfect day."

"That's how I often feel, too."

"Meagan's coming over for dinner tonight, so I've got lots to do."

"You lucky dog. From what you've told me, she sounds pretty special. It'll be good to have her company for an evening – just an evening, right?" He sniggered. "Well, anyhow, I called to ask you if you wanted to go to the pub for dinner tonight, but you've certainly got a better evening planned. By the way, does Meagan have a brother or relative living here?"

"Why do you ask?"

"I was having a drink at the Lighthouse the other night with one of the people I work with and I heard this guy sitting near us mention the name Meagan. It leapt out at me because of your Meagan. Then he said something about her being really pissed, which, as you know, can mean drunk or angry. I couldn't hear anything else he said."

Brad felt a rush of concern. "What did he look like?"

"He had blondish hair, looked fairly respectable, but a real loudmouth."

"Well, someone like that wouldn't get near Meagan."

"I didn't think so. Okay, talk to you later."

As he washed and sliced vegetables, he mulled over what he had heard. It kept going through his mind that it probably had been Will doing the talking, and simply being a loudmouth as usual. If Will barges in on Meagan again, I'll have a serious talk with him.

By five o'clock, the Greek salad had been made, and the salmon filets were lightly seasoned for cooking. On the stove, a pot of water sat ready for heating. With time to relax, he sat on the sofa contemplating the evening ahead with Meagan. To the gentle and moving tones of Mendelssohn's "*On the wings of song*," he thought again about how he'd felt when they'd worked together in her kitchen. Each time their eyes met had been a stirring allurement; she must have felt it, too. Being with Meagan gave him a feeling of comfort, like he'd never be misunderstood. He surmised she played the game of life in a positive way and, perhaps, the game of love as well. He imagined being with her and feeling her love every day.

Chapter Fifteen

Meagan arrived for dinner looking as fresh as if she had just come from a spa. Now, seeing her in his home, Brad was even more captivated by her beauty as she entered the house in a poised, almost balletic way.

"Hi Meagan, it's great to see you," he said, expecting to give her a hug as he did with Alexis, but she seemed not to anticipate it.

"It's great to see you, too. It's been such a long time," she happily replied.

In the living room, she stopped and looked around. "This is really nice. I can see you've got good taste. This doesn't look like a man cave to me. No stalactites here."

He laughed. "I saw them off when company's coming. (He gestured) Have a seat on this recliner. Would you like a glass of wine?"

"Yes, thank you, Brad."

As he walked to the kitchen, she appraised his physique, so manly from every angle. Being near him again had already begun to warm her feelings, as it had the last time they were together at her house.

When he returned with the drinks, he set them on the small table between his cream-colored leather recliners that had been turned inward to enhance conversation.

When they were comfortably seated, he looked at her over the rim of his glass and felt a soulful kind of exhilaration he hadn't experienced before in quite the same way.

She had a sip of wine and looked around the room. "How big is your house?"

"It's a fairly modest sixteen-hundred square feet, big enough to have everything I wanted."

"That's really big compared to my eight-hundred-and-fifty square feet, and it seems perfect for me. But I do have to get more done before it's the way I want it."

She had another sip of wine. "This wine is very nice. How did you know I liked Sauvignon Blanc?"

"A little bird told me."

She smiled. "I'll bet I know that little bird."

He chuckled and nodded. "She phoned to chat the other day and told me about having completed her Mexican house purchase and how it can now be scheduled for construction. She thought it would have been nice for us all to be there for the Christmas holiday."

"Now that I'm working at the store, I'm not sure I could or should go," she said as she sat back, pushing a strand of blond hair behind her ear. "In any case, it will be soon here and gone like any other day. I don't get stressed about what to do. In fact, I don't think it'd bother me to spend it alone. I'd go out and be with Mother Nature on a nice trail in the woods."

He raised an eyebrow in surprise. "You sound

like me. In fact, I've said much the same sort of thing myself."

"Alexis will be alright. She has friends who live near her property. She'll be perfectly happy to spend Christmas with them. In fact, she's been invited to stay with them until her home is completed. You've probably heard her say when it's built you're welcome to visit anytime."

"She has mentioned it."

"Do you think you'll go?"

He thought for a moment and shook his head. "It'd be nice, but I don't think so. I know the area well. Frankly, I have a new favorite destination … Cuba. I went there a few years ago and loved it."

"I'd like to see Cuba, too," Meagan said. "When I do visit Alexis in her Mexican home, it'd be a perfect jumping-off point."

"It'd be handy alright." (He looked at his watch) "You've been a working girl all day, and it's no doubt past your normal dinner time, so I'll go to the kitchen and heat the water for rice. The salad is made, and the fish won't take long."

"Should I come to the kitchen with you? I could be your sous-chef if needed."

He grinned. "Okay, so long as you don't steal any of my cooking secrets."

He put the pot of water on the burner, set the heat, and looked at her. "I've wondered why you bought a house instead of a condo."

"I was tired of living in a condo," she said as she stepped beside him. "I rented one for a short time before coming here, but I didn't like being surrounded by other people's sounds and activities. My place is bigger than some of the condos I looked at, plus it has the privacy and space a yard provides. My marriage settlement and some investments meant I could afford what I wanted, and the price was right. It provides me with a cute place near the ocean, with no mortgage and money in the bank. That's important to me."

"You did well," he said, adding brown rice to the almost boiling water. "Wow. So you like brown rice, too. It's my favorite, and so much more nutritious than white rice."

"You're right. It's full of important vitamins and minerals. And it tastes, at least to me, better than the white," he said as he stirred it, turned down the heat, and placed the lid on the pot. "Now let me show you around."

Downstairs, Meagan was impressed with his belongings, the large barrister bookcase, the paintings, and the metal castings of dancers and animals, especially the magnificent brass horse that was a cast reproduction of an ancient Chinese Han Horse.

The upstairs rooms told yet more about him and his sensibilities. She couldn't help being impressed by the tasteful appointments. In the bathroom, she admired the glassed-in bathtub and shower and the large medicine cabinet with two bottom drawers, which made it handier than most medicine cabinets she had seen.

“Where did you get that fabulous medicine cabinet? I love those drawers. Talk about convenience.”

“It came with the house and impressed me, too.”

The master bedroom quickly caught Meagan’s attention, from its furniture to artwork. A couple of large paintings were outstanding for their imagery and color. He definitely likes nice things.

“I like your paintings. They’re an inspiration for me to upscale the decor in my own home. But your way can be a bit expensive.”

“Only if you let it. Start slow and know what you're buying.”

Dinner preparation continued to occupy his mind, albeit in a distracted way. Returning to the kitchen, he gazed at Meagan, momentarily transfixed by her hazel eyes that could, depending on the light, show shades of green and brown, with hints of gold. Hers showed a dramatic shade of green and gold that was hypnotic. They drew him closer. He wanted to get closer still, to uncover her veiled essence.

She stood, looking at the counter and its dinner preparations. “Let me know what I can do to help if you need it.”

“I’d love your help. I forgot to chop the garlic. Would you mind?”

“If you don’t mind me smelling like garlic all evening.”

He chuckled. “I love the smell of garlic.”

She washed her hands, peeled and chopped several cloves, and washed her hands again. He began warming the frying pan and adding olive oil. He tore off a paper towel, wiped some olive oil from the counter, and looked at her.

“I never thought I’d be lucky enough to have a sous chef.” He smiled. “And I’m glad it’s you.”

She warmly returned his gaze. “And you were a good sous chef at my place.”

At that moment, an uplifting piece of music played on the stereo. Brad reached out to her, and she took his hand. They were quickly swirling in a Rachmaninoff dance of lightness and romance, like a couple who did it often.

“Wow. That’s exactly what I thought it'd be like to dance with you,” he said excitedly as he looked deeply into her eyes. “You’re a wonderful dance partner.”

“You surprised me with your dancing. You’re a wonderful partner, too.”

“We’ll do it more often, I hope.”

Meagan nodded her agreement.

As Brad put the salmon filets and chopped garlic in the frying pan, both chef and sous chef became increasingly aware of the ramped-up effect of their closeness. Accelerated by the dance. This dinner together wasn't about his repairs on her house and her reciprocating meals. It had a more intimate reason, an opportunity to simply be together and get to know each other. He sensed she was still in no hurry to take things to another level. He knew there had to be a reason. But what was it? They were nevertheless on a similar track, in spite of scant revelation about destination or time of arrival.

He moved the pot from the burner as she stood looking amused.

"I'm glad you like brown rice. I like it, too, for the same reasons you do. It's very convenient to have a pot of rice on hand and then heat up a portion with other things added to it. Perfect for busy people."

"It's done," he said as he lifted the lid and stirred the rice. "You're right, it's great with almost everything and it gets my creative side going. You wouldn't believe some of the dishes I've created."

When dinner was on the table, they sat across from each other, smiling with the fact of their togetherness and maybe even wanting to be closer.

Brad certainly.

“This is terrific, Brad. You can not only fix things, you can cook as well. The salmon’s texture and flavor are wonderful.”

“I like to cook, but I’m not a slave to it. As for the rest, I guess you could say I have an organized mind. I like symmetry, but I’m not OCD … I don’t think so.” he snickered. “And I remember having this conversation in your kitchen when I was slicing tomatoes.”

She laughed. “Well, you might be a trifle OCD, and perhaps me, too. Alexis says I’m obsessive-compulsive because I like to have my clothes closet and shoe racks so organized. Everything in its place according to what the need will be – indoors, outdoors, formal, informal. And speaking of clothes, even though I've two closets, they weren’t even close to what I needed. I ended up giving a lot of things to a thrift store."

He nodded knowingly. "Me, too, when I moved here."

Dessert time arrived. Brad set it on the table with a flourish and announced, "Chocolate cheesecake."

"Oh, one of my favorites," she enthused. "You remembered I like chocolate."

"Yes, and I do, too. In fact, I sometimes think I'm a chocoholic."

They happily finished with dessert and then walked to the living room where they drank tea in an aura that encouraged them to relax and open up to each other.

He looked at her fixedly. "Ever since I met you, I've been reminded that you're a city girl. And it makes me wonder how you'll adjust to living in a small town. Mind you, I'm having the same experience, but I think it's easier for a single man than it is for a single woman."

She slowly nodded. "In some ways, I suppose, but starting a new job in an industry I know well is a big plus, and especially makes working with a long-time friend. What about your plans?"

Brad shrugged. "I can take my time to figure out what the next step is. I have some fallback positions to consider and one of them is freelance writing. I've recently taken steps in that direction. Of course, I wrote advertising and business material for my magazine."

"Being retired, you're fortunate to have things you enjoy doing," she said, pointing. "Such as collecting antiques like yours. They're beautiful. Perhaps you could give me a tutorial on antiques someday."

He put down his cup. "The first thing to be aware of is that there are many fakes and reproductions. You have to be careful. Do you have an interest in particular antiques?"

She shook her head. "Not in a knowledgeable way, but I can appreciate them. In fact, I do have a nineteenth-century, silver pocket watch that belonged to my great grandfather."

"Now that is interesting. I'd like to see it sometime."

Their discussion about antiques collecting included her mentioning her ex-husband Adam's passion for sports collectibles. Her comment opened a window to her married past, something he had been wanting to know more about.

"You and Adam were married for quite a few years. You had no children?"

She thought for a moment. "The reason is that I had a chromosomal irregularity that made me infertile. I'd have agreed to adopting a child, but he wanted no part of it. He wanted a child that would be his own. His immovable stance meant we were in a no-win situation. I had become an impediment to his expectations. As time went on, he became more critical of me. Eventually, I heard of his involvement with a woman at his real estate office. I confronted him; he denied it. So I hired a private detective and got the proof. I got a divorce last year, and because there were no children involved, I changed back to my maiden name, Atherton."

"Would you have liked to have children?"

She sipped her tea, put down her cup and said, "I'm sometimes asked that. To be completely honest, I've never felt I needed offspring … but maybe if I was with the right man. Why," (she smiled) "are you looking for a woman with whom to start a family?"

He shook his head, glad for the opening. "No, my last relationship ended because I didn't want to start another family, and she did. So you and I have a convoluted similarity in circumstances."

She nodded thoughtfully. "I got married a bit late at thirty-one, and eventually reached a point where I wasn't sure myself if I wanted to begin starting a family, partly because of deteriorating aspects in my marriage."

"I already have a daughter. And though it's fairly common to see an older man starting another family, it's usually with a much younger woman. He can be a daddy and have his young and attractive trophy wife to show off like arm candy."

"How much younger than him would the woman have to be to be considered arm candy?"

He thought for a moment. "It's all about perception. You could be arm candy for any man at any age."

"Thanks, but I'd want to be more significant than arm candy. And while we're on the subject of breakups, tell me more about yours."

He looked at her, hesitating for a moment. "What I'll say about my situation with Karen, just so you'll understand, is that we came to realize we had entirely separate goals. She wanted to marry and have children, but I didn't. Trying to talk through it only widened the abyss between us. It finally became so stressful, so unsolvable, we decided on a trial separation, and that ended it."

She could see his sensitivity and sincerity that confirmed what she already saw in him. She thought about her own similar feelings. "Well, it looks like we've been on similar tracks."

"Two peas, separate pods. And now here we are, two viable and healthy plantings in Mother Nature's amazing seaside garden. I'd say we're pretty lucky to be here, wouldn't you?"

She looked at him appraisingly and replied, "We are lucky."

He wanted her to acknowledge that they were on a similar track together. It had been obvious from the start that they were attracted to each other. This evening, their looks at each other said their hearts were filling and each wished to be confirmed in the heart of the other, free of needless restraints whatever they might be. But when he twice tried to approach her with a look of wishing to somehow be closer to her, she chose to ignore it. Her control made him suspect there was a logical reason she had yet to tell him about.

Nevertheless, he felt he'd do almost anything to get some reaction from her. She was so different from her touchy-feely sister. He thought, before she leaves tonight I should hold her and try to get some kind of reaction one way or another.

What he couldn't know was the extent of her feelings for him. Sometimes when she looked at him she thought that time will soon reveal to him what she feels – meanwhile, please know that I love you.

As the evening was winding down, he said, "Meagan, I enjoy the times we spend together. Perhaps I can take you hiking on some of the trails around here."

"I'd like that. I haven't spent any time on them

and have meant to."

"None of them are far away. I'll call you for some hiking; in fact, how about next Sunday?"

She thought about it and enthusiastically replied, "Wonderful, but not in the morning. Especially on Sundays, I like a slow start to the day."

Saying that, she looked at her watch. "Wow, eleven-thirty. It proves time does fly faster when a good time is being had. I've really enjoyed the evening and your wonderful dinner."

"You don't have to go yet, do you?" he said.

"It's late, and Alexis and I are going to Gibsons for lunch tomorrow. I probably won't get to bed for another hour."

He stood and offered his hand. "I've enjoyed having you here this evening. We'll do it again soon, okay?"

She took his hand and stood up. "Yes. I'd love to."

They walked toward the door, both aware that there could have been more togetherness to the evening. He was certain that she felt it as he did.

At the door, she stood facing him, her eyes not leaving his.

“Thanks again for a lovely dinner and with such good company,” she said, smiling.

“I very much enjoyed your company as well,” he said. “The time passed much too quickly. We need more time to get to know each other better. I care about you.”

“That’s a nice thing to say, and I feel the same way about you. But first, I have to more fully get to know myself. I went through a psychologically rough time in my marriage and I’m still getting over some of it. So please be patient with me. We met only a short time ago and can afford to give it time. We’re fortunate to meet at this stage of our lives and can knowledgeably discuss such things.”

Brad nodded thoughtfully and opened the door. But before he could say another word, Meagan laid her hand on his arm. “Don’t give up on me, Brad.” Then, so saying she bid him good night and left.

Later, as he lay in bed, he thought about how different the sisters were. Alexis happily threw attention at him, but they were a shallow pond of affection, easily passed off. He surmised Meagan wanted deeper waters. She wasn’t simply being coquettish. He would be patient — and anticipate the feel of her lips on his.

Chapter Sixteen

On Monday morning, Brad had barely finished his second cup of coffee when his phone rang. A cheery woman identified herself as Emma Holt, editor at The Coast Journal. She asked if it would be possible for you to come by and have a chat sometime – perhaps even this afternoon? They agreed and met at the office at two o'clock. He found her to be eminently likable.

She was pleasant, with warmth and intelligence in her brown eyes, enhanced with a welcoming smile. He judged her to be somewhere around age forty. Her dark-brown hair, cut short and stylish, added to her savvy appearance. And her down-to-earth attitude was one he knew he could work with. He had known editors who were difficult, often because they wanted to be an editor in capital letters. She didn't appear to be that kind.

After introductions, she told how she had been with the paper for six years, had seen it through ups and downs, and won several industry awards. He gave her some of his background information, and in their discourse, he soon felt that with her at the helm things could be easily worked out as to how he'd fit in.

She laid out the reason for hiring a writer. "I'm looking for another writer because one of ours is moving back to Vancouver. He apparently misses the city."

He smiled. "Having seen the lifestyle here, I can't imagine going back to the rat race."

"I agree. I'm a coaster and plan to remain one. (she paused) So Brad, were the articles you sent me typical of your work, subject-wise and length?"

"They were pretty typical in the seven hundred to twelve-hundred-words range. Some, of course, would be longer."

"So what are you looking for exactly, staff or contract?"

He thought for a moment. “The last paper I wrote for was on contract, which I prefer. But it might help if I knew what you’re looking for to fill the job.”

Their discussion concluded with Emma contracting Brad to write a weekly business column with particular attention paid to the retail sector. In addition to the column, he'd write feature stories, especially special editions, when required. He’d not be a reporter covering such things as council meetings and accidents, nor would he be required to complete the column or stories at the newspaper’s office, a condition he specifically asked for because it could as easily be done at home. The job could start anytime. They agreed to the first Monday in September, and a contract was signed. Their meeting had gone well, and he left feeling it had been exactly what he had hoped for. As he drove away, he couldn't help feeling a bit pressed at the thought of being again in harness.

Arriving at home, he felt it might begin to make

him more keen about having a job if he told someone about the reality of his employment. Before he decided who to call, his phone rang. He picked up and heard the cheery voice of Connie Megalos. "Hi Brad, are you busy?"

"Hi Connie, no not at the moment. I just got home. How are you?"

"I'm okay. I told Eric I was going to phone you even though he didn't think I should. He has a rush job with some heavy and expensive hardwood panels needing to be cut today. The trouble is they're four-feet long, three feet wide and difficult for him to hold steady on the saw table. One waiver, and the panel is ruined. I could do it, but my osteoporosis would make me pay for it. So I'm wondering if you'd have a few minutes to help Eric get this job done. There's only three panels. It wouldn't take long. All you'd have to do is hold one end of a panel to keep it steady and straight as it's being cut."

He looked at the clock. "I'd be glad to help. Do

you mean right now?”

“Yes, if you don’t mind. He’s waiting to hear what you say. Don’t tell him I said that.”

“Okay, Connie. I’ll put on my jeans and leave right away.”

“Thanks, Brad.”

Eric looked both pleased and apologetic when Brad walked into his shop. Brad assured him he was happy to provide a hand. And the timing couldn’t have been better.

“Well, it’s good of you, and much appreciated. These are the panels (pointing). They’re Desert Ironwood from Arizona. Brad scanned the shop. “You’ve got some amazing equipment here. So what can I do?”

Eric explained the process; it wouldn’t take long, and Brad could stay for dinner. His job would be to grip the panel as it neared the saw and press it to the side rail to keep it absolutely square and flat.

Eric would also guide it by pressing it against the rail at his end. So saying, he picked up a panel, laid it on the table, started the saw, and looked intently at Brad. "Okay, now we'll make the cut as we hold the panel real steady against the rail." Then slowly and carefully, they began. The cut went perfectly. Eric assured Brad the rest would be just as easy.

As the second board was being cut, its denser grain needed greater effort to guide it straight. At about a third of the way through the cut, Eric called out, "Press hard," and he quickly reached over beyond the blade to help Brad more strongly press the board against the rail. At warp speed, an undone cuff on Eric's sleeve was sucked into the whirling blade. He suddenly shouted and flung his hand into the air, throwing a spray of blood in a wide arc. Brad was horrified to suddenly see one of Eric's fingers lying and twitching on the table. He quickly grabbed a nearby shop towel, wrapped it around Eric's hand and, taking him by the arm, shouted, "Let's go," as he began leading him to the house.

"Connie," he called. "Eric's had an accident." She ran to the door and stood looking at the bloody towel, taking a moment to absorb what she saw.

"He's lost a finger," said Brad, breathlessly.

As Eric grimaced with pain, Connie put her arm around his waist and told him to hold his hand up to slow the blood flow as she led him to a kitchen chair and wrapped his hand in a larger towel.

Brad grabbed their wall phone, called 9-1-1 and handed the phone to Connie to provide the address. She was told to wait for an ambulance. It would provide medical attention onsite as well as en-route to the hospital. The operator also suggested putting the finger in a small, sealable plastic bag and placing it in a bowl of ice for the responders.

"The finger!" Brad said as he ran to the shop, turned off the saw and picked up what was one of Eric's little fingers; it looked upsettingly at odds with the surroundings as it laid there. Holding it between his thumb and index finger, he ran back and gave it to Connie who, only vaguely squeamish, did what was outlined by the 9-1-1 operator.

"Well, that was a stupid thing to do, wasn't it?" Eric said. "And look at this Mackinaw. A piece of the cuff is gone."

He stared at it wonderingly and looked up at Connie, standing beside him. "I need a drink."

She quickly returned with a small glass of ouzo.

He downed it in a gulp. "When I saw the cuff suddenly flap, the blade instantly caught it. If I hadn't reacted in that split second, it might've taken off a lot more than my little finger. So I guess I came away lucky."

He lifted the glass for Connie to pour another shot and raised his glass toward Brad, who shook his head.

"If there's a good side to this, it's better the little

finger than losing one or more of the others," Brad said, optimistically.

Eric nodded. "I guess so. But look at you. I'm sorry about that," he said, pointing.

Brad looked down at his shirt, seeing blood spots in a track across his chest looking like pointillist art. He had changed into jeans, but in his rush hadn't changed his blue-tone Hathaway shirt. "Well, so much for dressing up for the job. I'll soak it and throw it in the laundry when I get home."

He noticed that Eric's work pants hadn't escaped either. Connie stood beside Eric with her hand on his shoulder as he grimaced with pain and frustration. "You're going to have to take it easy for a while, dear. Maybe it's a good time to go on that Greek vacation we've been putting off."

"I can't think about that now. I've got to get those damn boards sawed, even if I have to send them out, which I'll probably have to do."

She hurried to the window. “I can hear the ambulance.”

“That’s one of the nice things about being in a small town. Nothing’s very far away,” Brad said as he dashed outside to give the driver a high sign.

When the ambulance pulled into the yard, the driver got out and quickly walked to the rear of the vehicle. He opened the door and, seeing Eric steady on his feet, lowered the step. A second person, a woman, approached, holding a small cooler. Eric met them with his wrapped hand enclosed in a plastic grocery bag to keep things tidy, Connie had said. She held a bowl of ice containing the finger in a small plastic bag.

The driver walked over, looked carefully at Eric, and said, “I’ll help you into the ambulance, and then you can lie down. It’s advisable after any kind of accident … and safer for you, too.”

The woman smiled at Connie as she took the bagged finger and placed it in the cooler. “You’ve done a good job, and I'll attend to it on the way to the hospital."

Eric had been safely strapped down, and before the rear door closed, Connie said, "I'll be down to the hospital soon, dear."

He waved and said goodbye and, looking at Brad, said, "Hell of a way to——" before the door slammed shut.

As the ambulance drove away, Brad and Connie walked back to the house. At the door, Brad said, "Is there anything I can do to help, maybe drive you to the hospital?"

She shook her head. "No, Brad, thank you. I'll drive there a bit later. It's been a heck of a day, and I'm sorry it's something you had to experience. I shouldn't have called you. But knowing Eric, he might've attempted to cut the boards himself, and who knows what worse things might've happened?"

At home, Brad felt exhausted. He began to

think about the events of the afternoon – one so good, the other so bad. Still, he optimistically felt that if the finger could be successfully reattached, or even if it couldn't, Eric would still be able to do his work.

As he relaxed, he thought about how his life would be changed with the new challenges soon to become part of his days. He looked at his watch – twenty minutes past six. Meagan should be home from work. He'd tell her about his new job and also try to warm things up between them. He wouldn't dwell on her pseudo standoff at his place but would instead make every effort to bring some better understanding to their relationship — what it is, isn't, or could be. He wouldn't assume one way or the other.

She, too, had thought hard about that night. It bothered her that she had been so seemingly confused about how to begin their relationship. She wanted to know how it felt to be in his arms. She'd have to be more relaxed, more open, and let it play.

It became front of mind when she picked up her phone. “I was just thinking of you.” He chuckled. “We obviously think alike. And I’m glad to be talking with you. I wasn’t sure if I should call.” She sensed his stress and was determined to begin anew. “Brad, I want to apologize for my attitude at your place. It can be hard to explain and —”

“Well, we can’t always be at the top of our game, although I was a bit taken aback. I thought I had misread you. In the time I've been with you, I've felt a connection, call it like-mindedness.”

“I feel it, too. So don’t be misled by my demeanor. We’re still getting to know more about each other.”

“We’ll just have to peel away some outer layers.”

“Get in a more relaxed mode,” she said, “So how was your day?”

“You won’t believe what happened. I received

a call from——"

"Before you continue, have you had dinner yet?"

"No, I haven't had time. It's been that kind of day."

"I'm making mushroom and sausage pasta. Why don't you come over for dinner and tell me about it when you get here?" He ran upstairs, had a quick shower, put on fresh clothes, and arrived at Meagan's place in little more than half an hour. She looked radiant as she opened the door.

He couldn't help grinning. "I don't know how you do it, always looking so perky."

"Perky? What does that mean exactly?"

"You know, fresh, energetic, huggable." And with that, he gave her a firm hug that surprised her.

"Wow. That was nice," she said, fully meaning it and wanting more of what she had for too long been denying herself.

He smiled. “There’s more where that came from. We’ll have to do it more often.” Dinner preparations were then put on hold as they sat on the sofa enjoying a glass of white wine – and their new reality. Their more comfortable demeanor quickly helped them to relax.

She leaned close to him. “So, tell me about your day.” He immediately felt the warmth of her nearness, so comforting after the horror of Eric’s accident. And what started as a heartfelt hug soon became an enticing awakening. They sat on her sofa as he went over the details of being hired by the newspaper and his positive feelings about it and then talked about helping Eric.

When he got to the part about his finger being severed, she put her hand to her face, “How horrible. It must have been awful to see.”

“It happened so fast … I suddenly saw the finger lying there. He’s lucky it wasn’t worse.”

“How was he after it happened?”

“Connie poured him a couple of shots of ouzo, and he appeared to be surprisingly calm. She was amazing, and I could tell it wasn’t her first time dealing with an urgent situation. They’re a great team. I called nine-one-one, and within minutes, the ambulance arrived. Everything went well.”

“I hope I can meet them one day. They sound interesting like nice people to be around.”

“They are, and they’d like you. You’re their kind of person.”

“Obviously, you’re their kind of person as well. And I think you’re my kind of person, too.”

She flushed, seemingly surprising herself at saying it. At that moment, something passed between them. As they looked into each other’s eyes, the room became suddenly electrified. At that point, she got up and walked to the kitchen, ostensibly to keep an eye on the dinner in the oven. As she left the room, he saw again what he had always admired: her overall attractiveness, the grace in her walk, and her tall, beautifully shaped figure, a modern-day Venus.

As she fussed in the kitchen, she began to think about what had made her feel so much affected and drawn to him. I think I love him. I know I love him. The past is the past. I need to get the present. Returning to the sofa, her color and calm restored, she said, “Tell me more about your new job.”

He told how he'd be a contract writer of a column and feature stories. The best part of it being he could do the work at home. It’d be a mostly daytime job, perhaps some evening interviewing, not a lot, no council meetings, and the like. Later, as they sat at the kitchen table having dinner, he noticed that she had finished painting the interior window and door trim in a lighter shade.

“Nice job on the trim,” he said. “Thank you. I wasn’t completely sure if I should go lighter or darker. I think the lighter shade looks good.”

“You’re right. It looks more stylish.”

"Brad, after seeing how well appointed and finished your place is, I wouldn't hesitate to ask your advice about interior decor matters. You've got good taste."

He chuckled. "Thank you. I'm glad you approve."

They laughed happily as they sat at the table. She had shown previously, as well as tonight, that she could cook and enjoyed meal preparation, unlike Alexis, who had said she wasn't a great cook and took little pleasure in it.

The meal was delicious, tastefully complemented with a Greek salad and Nanaimo bars for dessert. Will Hackett drove carefully as he headed home from the pub. He already had one DUI, and attracting any kind of attention would be the last thing he needed.

As he drove past Meagan's house, he slowed and scanned the property as he always did, hoping to get a look, even the briefest look at her. Instead, he saw Brad's Camaro parked beside her car. It surprised him, and he couldn't help feeling angry because he had met her first; he should have been her friend, not this smart-ass newcomer.

By the time he got to his house, he had worked himself into a fit of jealousy and possessiveness. He poured himself a beer and sat in front of the television to think about the situation. So tonight, he just happens to be in the neighborhood and at Meagan's house. *Dammit all.*

Chapter Seventeen

They had finished dinner and were leaving the table when Meagan said, “I’ll do these dishes tomorrow.”

Brad took her hand. “Why don’t we do them now?”

She looked at him with mirth in her eyes. “You want to do dishes?”

“I’ll help you. No use adding to tomorrow’s workload. And after a delicious meal like that, I almost feel like I should do them myself.”

“You mean it, don’t you?”

“I wouldn’t have said it if I didn’t. And when you have a volunteer helper, there’s no better time to do them. I’m lucky; I can put mine in the dishwasher.”

She looked at him appreciatively. “Okay, let’s do it.”

As she washed and he dried, they reveled in each other’s company, especially given their heightened feelings. Dishes done, she made Earl Grey tea, and they retired to the living room to watch television and the early progression of the Canadian election.

She started to change channels. “This is boring. Let’s listen to some music. What do you like?”

“Anything but rock ’n’ roll.”

She switched to a music channel. “Here’s something I like, and I think you will too.”

The room filled with the sensual sounds of a Viennese waltz. “Nice choice,” he said.

He stood up, bowed, and reached for Meagan’s hand. They danced closely, so closely that when the piece ended, they turned back to their tea, both needing to cool down.

“I enjoyed that,” she said. “I don’t meet a lot of men who can dance like you do.”

“Well, you danced like you were floating on air. Have you always been a dancer?”

“Yes, in fact, I studied ballet until I was nineteen.” He nodded knowingly.

“Alexis mentioned you were in ballet. And now you danced so lightly and smoothly.”

“We had to know how to do all kinds of dances because we were often called upon for backup in a variety of performances. Where did you learn to dance so well?”

“My mother taught me when I was in my early teens. I can remember placing my stockinged feet on top of hers while she made the dance moves until I could do them myself. She said she didn’t want a future daughter-in-law to complain that I didn’t know how to dance. (He grinned) Or do housework.”

She looked at him admiringly. “Well, I enjoyed that dance more than I've enjoyed one for a very long time. And you’re a good dish dryer, too.” He laughed.

“Gee, thanks. So why did you quit ballet?”

“I wanted to make a more long-term and

predictable living. So, I obtained a fashion marketing certification at Uvic and ended up managing a high-end women's clothing store in Vancouver. Now that I'm working with my friend Cindy in her clothing store, I'm sure our combined experience will make an even greater success of what she's started."

Her phone suddenly rang; she picked it up and said, "Hi, sis."

After an exchange of pleasantries, she explained that she and Brad were having an evening together and promised to call the next day. She put the phone down and said, "Alexis says hi."

To the strains of another Viennese piece, he again took her by the hand and into his arms. As he held her, he breathed in her essence, so feminine and enticing. With the same kind of awareness, she felt the power in his arms, his masculinity, and the sureness of his guidance on the floor, making her want more.

As they danced, body chemistry intensified and

burned in their veins. When the music ended, he looked into her eyes, framed her face between his hands, and pressed his lips to hers. “Oh, Brad," she sighed.”

He kissed her again and said, “The first time you and I were working in the kitchen together, I wanted to take you in my arms. And every time we’ve been together, I've longed to hold you.”

“You wonderful man, I have the same feelings for you. I've been putting the past behind me ever since I met you. I need … (tears welled in her eyes) … my confidence and … hold me.”

He held her close and felt her convulse with a sob. They tightly embraced as two people holding onto what now mattered most. He kissed her tears and covered her lips with kisses that were hotly returned. She gestured to the sofa. “Let’s sit down. I’m glad this day has come, and you’ve helped make it happen.”

He looked at her concernedly as she wiped her

tears. “Don’t be concerned. It’s simply that I find I’m still getting over some of the issues from my marriage that have made me feel unsure of myself, such as now. I told you about it before, but there’s more.”

Seeing his look of concern, she said, “I’m sorry——” He placed his hand on her arm and said, “It’s okay. I want to hear about it.”

She nodded slowly, looking into his eyes. “Even before it became clear that I could not have children, Adam had an attitude about roles. He was what could be called autocratic and to a hurtful degree. He wanted to have children, and when it became clear we wouldn’t, couldn’t, he became demeaning. He once said our marriage suffered because of it and shouted, ‘And whose fault is that?’

During that period, he actually accused me of being unfeminine damaged goods, all things that began making me feel less than a whole woman. You can have no idea how it feels to be so demeaned. I began to dwell on it, lost sleep, became chronically fatigued, lost confidence, and became despairing. I dwelt on it so much that I convinced myself I really was inadequate.

Then I heard he was having an affair with a woman at his office, and you know the rest." He put his arm around her. "You've come a long way since those days. When I met you, I knew you were here for a new beginning, to breathe the same fresh air I breathed. I could relate to you totally."

She reached for his hand. "By that time, I had arrived at a point of freedom from the stress of the past. When Alexis moved here, partly to support me, my life got even better. So by the time I met you, I thought I had it all together." (She held his hand more tightly) "Being more intimate with you is challenging my confidence, making me uncertain if I can be the woman you expect me to be."

"No matter what Adam may have said about you, you are a whole woman, the woman I love, the woman I want in my life."

"I am the person I've always been. I'm just feeling a latter-day sting of wounded confidence. I've cared about you since we first met, and I didn't want to mess it up. You only need to see how I look at you to know I love you," she said tearfully.

He nodded and kissed her. "And I love you, too. We can have our future together, a new beginning, and we know we don't have to rush into it." He again pulled her onto the floor, and they danced so close they felt as one. When the music stopped, she put her face up to him, and he captured her lips with kisses, her heart beating on his chest in a pulsing current that had too long been coiled and quiescent within her. In her eyes were the fires of liberated passions. At a dizzying point of arousal, she held his face between her hands, kissing him again and again. Then, as if starving for each other and could no longer hold back the tidal wave of pent-up passion, they, without another word, went hand-in-hand to the bedroom. Later, lying in each other's arms, Brad held her close as he pressed his lips to hers and kissed her deeply. "We've found a new world, our own love land."

"My darling, I love you so much. You've helped free me to be me."

Brad said, "We were simply meant to be together. We were made for each other."

She nodded. "And to think I was afraid this day might never come."

After lying there for a while, she said, "I think a candle would be nice. Would you like that?"

"I think a candle would be perfect."

From her bedside table, she withdrew a candle holder, a candle, and a lighter. She got up, lit the candle, and turned off the light. "I sometimes light a candle to relax in bed."

When he slid over momentarily to move the candle further from the bed, he noticed a large kitchen knife in the drawer but decided not to mention it.

Then, in their newfound other world, they lay in the enchantment of an afterglow as they watched the candle's dancing flame throw shimmers around the room. Then, after murmured discussion, she whispered in his ear, "Sweetheart, we'd better get some sleep. I have to go to work in the morning."

So saying, she got up, blew out the candle, and went to the bathroom before returning to lie in his arms.

In the kitchen the next morning, he brought up what he didn't want to mention the previous evening. "Last night, when you took out your candle, I saw a knife in the drawer."

"I'm sorry you saw it. I wasn't going to say anything about it, but there have been times when the sounds I heard at night made me feel quite scared."

"Meagan, this is Sechelt. Before I moved here, I checked the town's demographics and crime stats, and Sechelt has one of the lowest crimes against persons imaginable and is declining. Also, I'm less than five minutes away, and I could be here even in my pajamas if you phoned."

"What if, in your haste to get here, you were caught speeding?"

"Good point," he said, and they laughed as he prepared to leave.

As she walked with him to his car, she stopped and pointed. "Can you drive it like that?"

Brad saw that the driver-side rear tire appeared to be almost flat. He shook his head. "No, I don't want to take a chance of ruining the tire." In the car's trunk, he found the spare tire to be fully inflated.

He turned to her. "I'll change the tires. You go ahead and get ready for work. I'll call you tonight."

After giving each other a loving embrace and warm kisses, she walked into the house as he got busy. Then, with the tire changed and seeing nothing to indicate further abuse, he drove away.

By the time he arrived at home, he was more than ready for coffee. After enjoying two coffees and a shower, he received a text-mail from Connie: “Hi Brad. Just to let you know, Eric’s finger reattachment went well. Everything will be okay. He wasn’t ready to come home last night until almost eight o’clock. I picked him up, and we were both pretty tired by then. He’s resting now, and I’m going to make him a nice big breakfast. Eric will phone you later. Bye for now. Connie.”

While having breakfast, he thought about the previous night with Meagan and how they had shown their innermost feelings of love. Even as he sat there, he could feel it deep in his soul. The time had come for him to think differently about his previously held views regarding living his life only according to his rhythm. While his viewpoints may have seemed logical, even with Karen, they could now only be called self-indulgent and foolish. Of course, there had been extenuating circumstances that seemed reasonable in past times. But now, they no longer prevailed. The missing ingredient had been Meagan; he knew his life wouldn't be complete without her in it. She, too, had her own apotheosis: their love and synergy had put her in touch with a renewed essence of herself. For each of them, their love had been transformational.

Meagan went to work feeling more uplifted than she could remember, with a clearer view of herself and her future. Very much like Brad had experienced, and he had shown himself to be unlike any men she had known. He showed sincere love and affection, as well as heartfelt consideration. Exactly what she needed, as she and Cindy sat in the store having a morning coffee before unlocking the door, she talked about his understanding and empathy.

"He's patient and sensitive, even in the face of tears when I told him about the hell I went through with Adam. It's a major difference from my previous experience."

Cindy had her own relationship story. “I had a boyfriend once who couldn’t stand me showing any emotion that involved tears. He acted as if I had become some sort of seeping, untouchable alien, like he didn’t want to get any of the seepage on him. He reacted like that to other things that are best left unsaid. He was good at some things, but as a warm and sensitive man, he had no clue. God help the next woman who tries to deal with him. Brad sounds heaven-sent, a charismatic man who knows how to listen and understand … at least try. He comforts your emotions and can show his own. With a man like that, you shouldn’t have any problems.”

Meagan nodded. “It’s only a small part of what I experienced last night when Brad stayed at my place.”

Cindy smiled happily. “Oh, Meagan, I was wondering when it'd get more serious.”

Meagan raised her hand. “You’re the only one who knows. It’s kind of a secret until I tell anyone else.”

They soon finished their coffees and unlocked the door. Cindy had recently stocked a fall collection of long-sleeve, cotton-acrylic sweaters in a range of attractive colors – certain to appeal to women of all ages. She had placed an ad in the newspaper and looked forward to having a busy day.

Shortly before lunchtime, Meagan phoned Brad to inquire about how things went at the tire shop.

“Well, get this, Meagan, they found nothing wrong with the tire or valve stem. All it needed was air. Apparently, the air had been let out. I’m wondering who would do that. I've got one person in mind.”

“It’s not something I'd want to have to think about, and I can’t help being worried about someone letting air out of your tire while your car’s at my place. But it does make me think of someone you’re probably thinking of, too.”

“It points to someone who’s got an attitude and

would do it either for kicks or for spite. I don't see someone doing it for kicks. I think spite would be a more likely reason, and that makes me wonder how anyone could be so spiteful. All I can think of is the fact that Will seemed to think or at least feel like he has visiting rights to your place, and I was upset about it. If he —"

"But Brad, he never had any visiting rights. He walked by my place one day as I unloaded paint from my car. He said he had experience painting, and I agreed he could help Alexis and me do it. He had never before been in my house."

"I know, but I think he's getting even for me being there, and he's never invited. Just keep an eye out for anything unusual, and don't hesitate to call me."

"All right, sweetheart. I love you."

"I love you too, Meagan. Talk soon."

Late Wednesday afternoon, as he walked into

his house with a bag of groceries, his phone rang; "Yassas (hello), Brad. I'm back home from the hospital. The finger's sewn up; it's now a stubby because I lost one joint."

"Hi, Eric. I'm glad to hear you've kept the finger. I'd imagine it will be quite sore and stiff for a while."

"It's all of that, but it will bend from the joint at the palm and can still be used; at least, that's what the doctor told me. He said it will take about a month before I can do anything that approaches fully using the hand. By the way, the doctor was impressed with how well you and Connie took care of it and kept it in good condition. He didn't even put me under for the reattachment; just gave me a nerve block. He said most finger reattachments are performed that way. I felt nothing … at least not until today. The painkillers they've given me help keep it at bay."

"Even so, you probably won't be doing any heavy woodwork for a while."

"Nothing serious, but small jobs if I'm careful. I

can’t use the hand much now because it’s so wrapped up. I’ll have to call my customer and tell him his cabinets will be on hold for a while. He’ll be pissed off. Too bad you’re not into woodwork.” He chuckled. “I’d hire you to do the job.”

“Even if I was a pro like you, I couldn’t do it. I've got a job.”

He told Eric about his employment with the Coast Journal. Eric punched the air, saying, way to go and invited Brad to come for dinner.

“How about next Sunday? Bring a girlfriend if you have one. I know you haven’t been in town long, but a guy like you shouldn’t have any trouble meeting women.”

Chapter Eighteen

Alexis was going through a personal crisis: "Where is everybody?" She had called Brad, but only his phone answered. She thought about calling Meagan, but she'd be loath to talk much while at the store. She needed to talk to somebody – anybody. She had some problems regarding her house in Mexico. She had to talk about it for no other reason than to cool down. Yet there was another reason: she felt increasingly lonely and neglected. Everyone else seemed to have places to go to, things to do, and someone to do them with. She knew there could be times when things would be quiet, but this quiet?

Alexis decided to phone Meagan; she answered. "Hi, Meagan. It's your sister calling. This is just a quick call to suggest we get together for dinner. Maybe tonight?"

"Gosh, Alexis, I planned on having a quiet night."

"Please! I need some socialization, and it's about time we got caught up. I haven't seen you for a while. You can relax tonight, and I'll buy dinner. Your choice of restaurant."

"I have to think for a moment—"

"Come on, can you do it?"

"Yes … I guess I can do it."

"Great! I'll pick you up around six thirty. Looking forward to seeing you." Alexis always had ways of convincing people to see things her way, if not through plain talk, then also by providing incentives. Tonight's incentive convinced Meagan that dinner out would be more relaxing than spending time in the kitchen. Besides, she enjoyed time spent with her sister.

When Meagan arrived at home from work, she opened her screen door and stood back as a dozen red roses leaned toward her. She took them into the house and read the enclosed card: "Dearest Meagan – I knew the first time we spent time working together in your kitchen that we were the heart and soul of a love story. You have made me realize what I'd been missing. I love you so much, Brad Meagan got a vase from a cupboard, filled it with water, carefully tucked the flowers into it and gazed at them excitedly before again reading the card that so much mirrored her own feelings. She thought again about their first night of love-fueled passion and wished Brad could be with her now. She wanted to phone him, thank him for the flowers and have a heartfelt conversation, but she had only a few minutes to get ready for Alexis. She texted Brad, thanking him and said she'd phone him after her dinner with Alexis. She signed off, “I love you the same way, Brad. Hugs. Meagan”

The Buccaneer Restaurant and the Lighthouse Pub are in the same building on the south shore of Porpoise Bay. Tonight Meagan and Alexis were at the Buccaneer, what Alexis thought would be the quieter place in which to enjoy dinner and conversation.

The Fall evening being too cool to sit on the deck, they sat inside at a table-for-two near a large window having a view of the bay and the Fall colors of the forest. They were two sisters, one of them an attractive middle-aged woman who held forth in a commanding and excited way, the other a somewhat younger woman, the picture of beauty and health, who listened attentively.

As well as being sisters, they were friends and confidants. After ordering wine, Alexis leaned forward. “Miguel phoned to say the foundation framing has started and might be completed before Christmas. The rest of the construction won’t begin until after the holidays. And as if that isn’t bad enough, he said one of the companies he uses has had some kind of slow -own that has resulted in other people in the community being in the same kettle of fish as me. So it’s like a project on the never-never plan.”

“But you’ve got lots of time before your condo rental ends, and you said you can even add to the length of the term if it becomes necessary.”

Alexis nodded solemnly. “Even with completion now scheduled for some time in the new year, I can’t help being worried. I have to think about what needs to be done and what to do with some of my furniture. I need a secure timeline for clearing out everything and making arrangements for shipping some of my favorite pieces to Mexico. Others will have to be sold. That’s something I wanted to talk to you about. I know you like some of my things and I’m happy to give them to you, and you can give me some prep help on weekends.”

Meagan winced. “Of course I’ll help you, but I do have some social obligations, you know.”

“You mean with Brad?”

“Yes with Brad. We’ve gotten much closer, and tonight when I got home I found a dozen roses at my door and a very sweet card from him.”

“I've seen how attracted you are to each other and I’m happy for you. I couldn’t have chosen a better man for you.”

Meagan nodded thoughtfully. “He sincerely knows how to respect a woman’s thoughts and emotions, and at the same time be in touch with his own. Keep in mind he’s had a breakup that he feels he’s partly responsible for.” She paused, wanting to say more. “We had a nice time last night.”

Alexis smiled and batted her eyelashes. “Anything you can tell your sister about?”

Meagan touched Alexis’ arm. “Brad and I spent the night together.”

Alexis threw her hands up. “I suspected as much. I’m so glad you two have discovered each other and with the same feelings. It’s so wonderful it almost brings tears to my eyes. I’m so happy for you both. And by the way, you don’t have to tell me about Brad’s responsibility and sincerity; I know he's a gentleman. I've seen it in his interactions with us and other people, his ability to know what is the right thing to do at a given time, and how to do it. He’s a rare bird.

"Yes, he knows how to fly high and has flown to another challenge, a writing job."

She told Alexis about Brad's job with the newspaper. Then changing the subject, she said, "Don't be surprised, but I ran into Will the other day. When he fixed my lamp switch some time ago, he said if my car ever needs repairs to let him know. He'd look at it and give a diagnosis. He said women are sometimes taken advantage of in these matters. And I don't know a damned thing about car repairs. So I told him a light on my dash came on last week that wasn't there before. I looked in the owner's manual and it said to have the car looked at; it could be any number of things. Will said it's probably some kind of sensor. He came by one day after work and checked it out. He ended up replacing it for the cost of the part."

"Alexis, why would you want to have him messing around with anything of yours? You know he's a loose cannon."

“I have a very good reason – cost. I don’t want to be faced with a large outlay if Will can do it for less. He won’t charge for his time if it’s an easy fix like a sensor. You remember him and Brad talking about replacing sensors. Besides, unlike you, I don’t dislike Will. He has always been helpful, and when you get to know him a bit better you can see he is actually quite a gentle soul. He’s simply a bit impulsive and a tad obsequious, almost too willing to please.”

Meagan looked at Alexis fixedly. “Well, just make sure you don’t end up making too much use of his willingness to please or anything else. I wouldn’t trust him.”

“It’s partly about knowing how to control a situation, Meagan. I’m a strong, older woman and–”

“As in cougars?”

“No, not as in cougar,” Alexis declared sotto voce. “Let me finish. If a woman acts weak and silly, many men will try to take advantage of it. But behaving in a mature, friendly, confident manner shows what to expect and not expect. I think Will sees me as an older woman who demands respect, like his mother."

"But what if he doesn't respect his mother? I'm not sure Adam respected his mother. He never contacted her much at all. In fact, she often complained about his lack of communication. And if a man doesn't respect his mother, can he truly respect other women? Brad very much respected his mother, and I've felt the benefits of it ever since I met him."

"Well, I don't want to psychoanalyze Will. I just want him to fix my car and save me some money. My Mexican venture will be expensive."

Meagan nodded. "I can well imagine the costs, and I'll do whatever I can to help you. And now (looking at her watch) I see it's getting late, and I've some things to do before bedtime."

The sisters had, as usual, enjoyed dinner and their time together. It was an occasion to, among other things, reminisce about life situations and people they both knew in Victoria. When they left the pub and walked to Alexis' car, Meagan became anxious, "I can't wait to get home and call Brad to thank him for the flowers."

"Don't worry," Alexis said. "I won't hang around. I'll drop you off and go home."

At Meagan's house, they embraced like the loving sisters they were, and Alexis drove home happily soothed by their evening spent together.

Meagan looked again at the flowers before phoning Brad. He answered her call with a cheeriness that spread a smile on her face. "How's my favorite coaster?"

"Wow, Brad, that's quite a moniker. It made me think for a moment. Yes, I am a coaster, like you."

"What could be better than you and me enjoying life together on the Sunshine Coast?"

"I can't think of anything better, and darling I

want to thank you for the lovely roses. They were a perfect pick-me-up at the end of the day. Alexis and I enjoyed our dinner together. And now tell me how was your day."

"I had an easy day, got a few things done around the house, laundry and so on, and went for a long walk. And I had a call from Eric. He said his finger feels better every day. He also invited us to dinner tomorrow. Gosh, Sunday already. It's kind of short notice, but I hope you can go with me."

She thought for a moment. "Yes, I'd love to. I'm looking forward to meeting Eric and Connie."

Chapter Nineteen

On Sunday morning, after breakfast, Brad went for a long walk around Sechelt Marsh. He wanted to have some time in the natural world to think about the job he'd start the following day. It'd be an abrupt change from his usual days since arriving in Sechelt, most of them enjoyable and satisfying. The best ones were spent with Meagan. As for his job, he had yet to buy an appointment book, something he forgot to do. There were adjustments to make, such as having the coffee maker ready to turn on in the morning or setting it on automatically. These things and others more mundane were what he now thought about. But today, he had little more to think about than having dinner with Meagan at the Megalos'. He could not, however, help thinking about Leonard Mason being released days ago. He thought *I'd like to have a face-to-face with him and settle things. For damned sure, I'll keep tabs on him and his whereabouts.*

For the evening at the Megalos', Brad took a

bottle of Okanagan's VQA Sauvignon Blanc wine and a bottle of ouzo to help sooth Eric's recovery. As he and Meagan drove there, she excitedly asked questions about the couple. Some he could answer, others she could ask.

Arriving at the house, they were met by Apollo. Brad patted his head. "Hi, Apollo, this is Meagan." Seeing his gentle manner, she also bent and patted his head.

Then Eric opened the door, saying, "Yassas, and who is this goddess you've brought with you?"

"Hello, Eric. I'd like you to meet Meagan." (and gesturing) "Eric."

Connie came to meet them, drying her hands on her apron before introducing herself to Meagan. Brad handed his bagged bottles to Connie while Eric led them into the living room.

When they were seated, Eric stood smiling, with his hands on his hips, one hand noticeably bandaged. “What say we have a drink?”

Connie came from the kitchen. “Brad has brought wine and ouzo.”

“*Ouzo*?”

“Medicine to help heal your finger,” Brad said, “Which, by the way, I’d like to see. It should help remove my last image of it.”

Eric laughed heartily. “Absolutely, but first,” (looking at Meagan), “what will you have?”

“I’ll have some of Brad’s wine.” Then, looking at Connie, “Perhaps you’ll have some as well.”

Connie nodded, “Thank you, Meagan.” “And you, Brad?” Eric said.

“I’ll have some of the ouzo I brought and invite you to join me. You can tell me what you think of it.”

“I’ll help with the drinks,” Eric said as he walked to the kitchen. Seeing the ouzo bottle, he looked around the corner at Brad. “That’s good ouzo. Barbayannis Aphrodite is one of the best.”

"I had some help from the store manager."

When the drinks were served, and everyone sat comfortably, Eric raised his glass, "Yamas, to health."

After the toast, Connie happily looked at Brad. "I'm so glad you brought

Meagan. Have you known each other for a long time? How did you two meet?"

He told how it began with meeting Meagan's sister Alexis in a thrift store's book section and then meeting Meagan at her house on painting day.

Connie said, "Well, it sounds like it was meant to be, and we hope to see more of you two."

Meagan smiled. "Thank you. I'll look forward to that."

"Of course," Brad intoned and looked at Eric, "So are you going to show us the new finger architecture? I can't help wondering how it's coming along after reattachment."

Eric raised his hand. “It’s surprisingly well-behaved and (he laughed) much smaller. Here, I’ll show you,” he said, undoing the wrap and removing the splint.

The finger showed good color, a neatly-stitched incision and little evidence of the violence it suffered.

“Wow, that looks pretty good,” Brad enthused.

Eric nodded. “You were probably expecting something gruesome. The entire reattachment process surprised me how well it went and how clean the finished result is.” He wiggled the stump. “So what do you think?”

“We live in a wonderful age in a very special country,” Connie said. “There are so many other places where you’d never have a finger reattached or anything else.”

Brad nodded. “I’m amazed. I expected to see it looking red and swollen. Is there any pain at all?”

"Only when I forget and try to grab something or bump it. Nothing serious. When I go back to work, I'll have to learn to compensate. It has a good feeling in it, which will be important. And when completely healed and exercised, it'll get stronger. It shouldn't affect my work much at all."

"The repaired cuff will be a good start to it." Connie shook her finger at Eric. "No more accidents."

Eric raised his glass to her. "Connie did a great job fixing it."

"Well, it's the least I can do to keep you in one piece."

"I thought I might've taken a week or two off work, but I think I can finish those panels in a few days and get on with the rest of the work," Eric said. "My neighbor has agreed to give me a hand with them. And for that, I'll repair the cracked leg on his antique desk."

"If you happen to get stuck on a piece of shop

work, I might be able to lend a hand," Brad said.

"Well, that's good of you. But I should be okay. Anyhow, that's enough about me. Tell us about your new job."

Brad talked about the kind of writing he'd be doing. The Journal wanted specific categories of stories and a new business column. "Perhaps now that I'll be writing for the newspaper, I could write about your business and help bring in some new customers."

Eric had a sip of ouzo and raised his glass. "This ouzo's good. As for more business, what I have now is perfectly adequate. We're in good shape. Nothing fancy, mind you, but enough for necessary expenditures."

"I'm beginning to know more about necessary expenditures," Meagan said. "Basically home repairs, like the ones Brad has so generously done."

"Well, you're lucky, and so were we with Eric's help," Connie said. "When we bought this place, it needed a lot of things done, things that he could take care of. We soon discovered there were mice in the house. There must have been an opening for them to get into. Eric checked the walls at the foundation and found a small gap in a board between the studs. Before the mice were completely eradicated, I one day saw Eric in the kitchen wetting the tip of his finger to pick up crumbs from the counter, and because I had seen a mouse on the counter earlier that day, I told him he'd better be sure of what he's eating."

When the laughter subsided, Eric said, "I caught three mice in two days. Soon, there were none left."

Meagan became curious. "So what did you do with dead mice?"

"I flushed them down the toilet."

"Weren't they too big to flush?"

Eric grinned. "I've flushed bigger things than that."

Eric and Brad guffawed. Meagan smiled and

looked at Connie, who, having heard it before, shook her head and changed the subject. “Meagan, where’s your house located?”

“It’s on Crayfish Avenue. It’s a smaller home, but certainly big enough for me.”

“What do you plan on doing to it?” Connie said.

“The exterior has been painted, and most of the interior. Brad has done some fix-ups, like new cupboard hinges, and he fixed my leaking kitchen faucet. There will be a few more things to address, nothing serious.”

“Her sister Alexis invited me to join in on painting day, and that’s when I met Meagan,” Brad said happily. “A momentous day for me.”

Meagan nodded. “For both of us.”

Eric raised his glass. “Here’s to good fortune.”

“To good fortune,” Brad said, sipping his ouzo. “As far as the rest of the house is concerned, as Meagan said, there isn’t anything really serious to be addressed. The smaller things I can fix. Fortunately, the roof's been done, and it has good bones."

Connie smiled. "Are we talking about a house or a living thing?"

"It means the house is solid, with a good framework, no bones deteriorating," Eric said.

Connie stood up and went to the kitchen. Returning, she said, "Come on, folks, it's time for dinner."

When they were seated at Eric's beautifully-made table, he poured everyone a glass of wine. Connie served one of her specialties: lamb shish kabob, with rice and a Greek salad. During the course of the meal, the conversation revolved around Brad's job and Eric's challenge at work, with a paw swipe or two given to Brad and Meagan's relationship. The meal ended with flan dessert and blueberries.

"The meal was delicious," Meagan said.

Brad seconded her comment, adding, "And the flan was a treat I haven't had since the last time I was in Mexico."

"I'm glad you liked it," Connie said. "We'll do it again."

Brad and Meagan had enjoyed the evening and looked forward to seeing them again. As he started the car and waved, Meagan said, "That was good of you to say you'd help Eric if he needed you."

"It wouldn't take long. Besides, it feels good to help someone in a fix. Have you ever heard the expression, *'Life will help you get what you want if you help others get what they want?'* It's another way of describing good karma, saying *do good, get back good.* I don't know who said it, but to me, it makes sense. And if giving and helping is pleasurable and rewarding, you're already getting back. Call it the power of giving."

Meagan stroked his knee. "Is that why you fixed my cupboards?"

He laughed. “It was about even more than helping you. I wanted to spend time with you and love you to pieces.”

His hand reached for hers. “I wish we could keep the evening going, but, as you know, I have a new job to go to in the morning. I’m already feeling the restrictions of being employed. By the end of this week, I’ll have a routine started that will make it easier to plan things. You and I’ll have to do some hiking on our days off. I’m looking forward to showing you some of the better trails.”

Stranding at the door of her house, he held her close as he looked into her eyes. “I’m already missing you. As I said, I wish we could keep the night going, but we have lots of time to look forward to.”

She nodded. Each of them knew their love wouldn’t be shown in a hurried way. It’d be a stronger touchstone than they ever anticipated.

When he arrived home, he sent a message to Chris telling him he wouldn’t be hiking because he had a writing job at the Journal. He also apologized for canceling the pub meet-up in favor of Meagan's dinner, something he'd never normally do.

He had reached the top of his stairs when his phone rang. He picked it up and heard an alarm in Meagan's voice. "Brad, I'm sorry to phone you so late, but I just now heard a light thump on my bedroom wall. And as a passing car went by, I saw a shadow move on my blind from the car's headlights. It looked like someone's head. I'm feeling a bit nervous about this, and I'm——"

"Meagan, hold tight. I'm driving over."

He parked his car at the end of the block and quickly walked to shrubbery near Meagan's house. Seeing nothing suspicious, he bent and quietly advanced to the rear of the house, aware that if someone lurked there, they might choose to fight rather than be caught. He had the skill and confidence to know he could handle most kinds of attacks, certainly hand-to-hand. But he knew people like Mason wouldn't be the type of person who'd fight conventionally. He reached the end of the wall and peered around the corner to the rear of the house. Nothing. At the next corner, he carefully looked around it to see the area near Meagan's bedroom window. Again, nothing. He then quietly walked to the front of the house and seeing nothing untoward, he backtracked to the bedroom window. "Meagan, there's nothing here. I'm going to walk over to Will's house and have a look. I'll be right back."

Will had been watching television and quickly opened his door when Brad knocked. "Well, what a surprise at this time of night."

"Just a friendly call to ask if you've been here all evening."

"Yeah, why?"

"Meagan called to say she heard someone or something moving around outside her house, so I'm trying to figure out who it could have been. I assume it wasn't you being out and about."

Will laughed. “You’re some detective, and you assumed right. What the hell do you think I’d be doing there at night like some kind of kook?”

“Will, I’m checking everything right now, rightly or wrongly, and I believe you. I’d appreciate it if you'd call me immediately if you ever see anything or anyone hanging around her house. Here’s my business card.”

Will looked at it. “Wow, so you’re writing for the paper.”

“That’s right. But listen, this is important and I’ll appreciate your help in letting me know if you ever see anything unusual around Meagan’s house.”

“No problem.”

“Thanks, Will.”

Meagan answered the door, looking tired but pleased to see Brad.

He wrapped her in his arms and kissed her. “I saw nothing near the house, and it wasn’t Will. He assured me of that and said he'd let me know if he ever sees anything suspicious going on."

"But what about the shadow?"

"A car passing someone walking on the road could throw their shadow. Was it a big shadow or a small one?"

"I could definitely see the outline of a head."

He knew without saying it, and she did, too, that that amount of outline detail meant the person must have been quite close to the window.

"Well, let's keep vigilant," he said. "And the next time you hear something, speak quietly on the phone so as not to spook whoever or whatever made the noise, and I'll dash over."

She held him tightly. "Thank you, darling." She looked up at him, "I wish you could stay."

"I do, too, my love. I'll call you tomorrow and tell you about my first day on the job."

They both felt the angst of parting and kissed

warmly. He then drove home, keeping his eyes peeled in all directions.

As he drove, he thought about Mason's prison release. *Anyone getting released from jail will have a load of things to do to get a normal life started again. There would be little reason to come to Sechelt and be a problem. After all, if I hadn't testified, someone else would have. But you'd have to know Mason. I well remember his pugnacious and vengeful attitude.* Brad wouldn't tell Meagan about it and needlessly put her in a worried state.

Chapter Twenty

It had been a restless night. In the morning, as he drove to the Journal for his first day of work, he noticed a small white car following some distance behind him. It wouldn't have seemed significant if it hadn't been there every time he looked in his rearview mirror. Whether it be a coincidence or trouble, it instantly put him on high alert. When he parked in front of the Journal's offices and got out of his car, the white car pulled up behind him. When its door opened, he couldn't believe what he saw. Outstepped Leonard Mason.

In his right hand, he held what appeared to be a club in the form of a wooden chair leg. Mason walked quickly toward him and screamed, "I'm going to teach you a lesson, Webster." He then lunged and swung the club at Brad, who instinctively dropped into a karate defense stance and blocked it so effectively that the weapon spun from Mason's hand and fell to the ground. It was followed by a punch that only grazed Brad's left cheek. He blocked another punch with an outside block and then another punch with an inside block. Then Brad attacked, delivering a snap punch to Mason's face. Mason staggered back a couple of paces and renewed his attack, his eyes glaring with the male violence of a wild animal. As he lunged forward, Brad saw an opening and delivered a liver kick, something so painful it could drop attackers to their knees. But nothing happened. The moment was suddenly frozen by an otherworldly sound. Brad struggled, opened his eyes and saw his alarm clock noisily chiming 6:30 a.m. He climbed out of bed, muttering a *hell of a way to start a new job*, and headed for the shower.

A few minutes before eight o'clock, Brad stood at the door of the Coast Journal's office wearing his work-a-day clothes: a pale-blue shirt, a navy blue blazer, pale grey slacks and no tie. He opened the door and, seeing no one, went to Emma's office. He looked in. "Good morning, Emma."

She looked up and thought, *Good looking and good writing, lucky me.* "Good morning, Brad. I should have told you we don't get into gear around here until eight-thirty. Do come in. I'll make coffee. When everyone's here, we'll have our regular Monday morning meeting, and after that, you and I can go over aspects of your startup."

At the meeting, he was introduced, and the usual business issues were dealt with. Then, with renewed coffees, they returned to Emma's office. When they were seated, she had a sip and put down her cup. "For the first week or so, I'll give you suggestions about the kinds of businesses to contact. You can take it from there. Let's keep it strictly business-oriented unless something directly related inspires more. Have you thought about the column's name?"

He shook his head. "Some names came and went, but I'd definitely like the word 'business' in it."

"Good idea. How about a photo? Do you have

a recent one you'd like to use? If not, we can take one."

"I have one taken in my Vancouver office this year. Also, what about business dress? Does what I'm wearing fit the Journal's code?"

Emma smiled and nodded. "You look fine. Ties are optional, but of course, there are times when it will be advisable to wear one, such as in a conference environment or some special business event," she paused. "You haven't told me much about your magazine."

He told how he started it, sold it and why, without relating to his personal side. The rest of the morning dealt with details regarding the sorts of material he'd be writing. After a discussion about the column, the name they agreed upon was "Coastal Business."

At noon, Emma suggested they go for lunch – her treat – to review what had been discussed and to be certain nothing of importance had been overlooked. She also wanted to know more about him.

Seated at “Coast Kitchen,” a popular newcomer to the local restaurant scene, she ordered halibut and fries; he had a bacon, lettuce and tomato sandwich with fries.

Emma looked pleased and comfortable. “I like this place. Have you been here before?”

“No, but I've been meaning to give it a try. I like their sign with the chef’s thumb up. Very positive.”

As they waited for their entrees, she opened up to enquire about what she wished to know about him, not all of it business-oriented.

“I know you haven’t been in town long, and you being from the city, I’m curious how you’re enjoying our quiet little burg.”

“The more quiet atmosphere is exactly what I wanted after years of doing business in Vancouver,” he explained. “Not only the quiet but also the beautiful natural environment that is so calming. I've started hiking with a group every week … at least I *was* hiking every Monday. But now I'll do it on weekends or evenings. I also want to get more involved with the community. I've always liked to volunteer for this and that and be multidimensional."

She smiled. "Good way to put it. So you bought a house and lived alone?"

"I've lived alone since my divorce and have always enjoyed a certain amount of solitude that suits the rhythm of my needs, things that are important to me."

She raised her eyebrow. "Such as?"

He laughed. "Such as doing what or when at my pace. And as far as living alone is concerned, exponential numbers of people are choosing to live alone. Though it might sound self-absorbed, I *am* a social person, and I'll know when the time comes to be more inclusive. What about you?"

She looked at him quizzically. “Me? I've lived alone since my husband and I split up three years ago.”

“Are you divorced?”

“No, and I don’t know where he is. I guess I could track him down, smoke him out, as George Bush would say, but a divorce isn’t going to pave the way to anything particularly important. Like you, I’m happy in my own skin. I'd imagine you’ve had an attachment since your divorce.”

He put down his cup. “I had a relationship with a good woman in Vancouver, but it ended before I came here. Different expectations… She wanted marriage and children. I’d been previously married and have a daughter. I’m not going to start a family again at my age. As time went by, she thought I’d change my mind. And here I am alone.”

She nodded. “And you’ve decided to go to work. Good for you. I like the articles you’ve shown me. I think we’re on the same page.”

Throughout their conversation, he noted her remarkable acumen regarding such things as his column, business features and business in general. Everything about her indicated an ambient reliability that made him feel confident and eager to get started. A server arrived with their orders, and lunch continued with light banter until it became time to return to the office.

Later, when he left the office, he bought some office materials, including a day timer. At home, he felt fatigue he hadn't experienced since his days at the magazine, the kind that led him to lie quietly on the sofa. It had been one of his luxuries and reminded him of William Wordsworth's words: *For oft, when on my couch I lie, in vacant or in pensive mood, they flash upon that inward eye, which is the bliss of solitude.*

Brad's father had always enjoyed knowing apt quotations such as this one, and Brad had learned to appreciate them, too. Handy summations.

After a short rest, he phoned Chris to talk about his first day at the Journal. Chris didn't have much time to chat; he had to deal with a woman whose dog had a painful bulge in its hip. It'd need an X-ray. They agreed to have dinner at the pub on Wednesday.

Meagan wouldn't be home from work yet, and he didn't want to get into the habit of calling her at work, so he called Alexis instead. She always appreciated a call, often using it to make plans for things that would sooth her growing boredom. But he wasn't going to be dragged into anything, at least not tonight.

"Hello Brad, nice to hear from you," she gushed. "It's been awhile."

"Things have been busier than usual, Alexis. For one thing, I've got a writing job at The Coast Journal."

"Congrats. Meagan told me," she replied.

"Today was my first day, mostly getting

organized and sorting out story prospects. The editor is helpful, a nice woman named Emma. Nicer than some of the editors I've known who like to spell the word "editor" with flashing lights. They often make work more difficult. I've pretty much given up on accepting unwarranted stress in my life. I've now become more of a lover than a fighter." He snickered.

She laughed. "Oh, you devil. How do you propose to test it?"

"It will happen in the most natural way possible in conjunction with the most special natural element of all."

"And what would the natural element be?"

"Even if you guessed it, I wouldn't tell you. It will happen when it happens, and then you'll see how it's meant to be. I'll let you know."

"You had me going there for a while. But I think I can guess what your special natural element is, and your secret is safe with me. I think you and the natural element make the right kind of combination for marvelous chemistry. After all, it's all about chemistry, isn't it?"

He smiled. "With the right ingredients."

"When I saw you two together at her place, I could see conductivity, a definite connection."

"Let's not get too far ahead of things, Alexis."

She laughed and said she and Meagan had been out for dinner, something Meagan had already told him. She went on to tell about a quick trip she made to Vancouver from sheer lack of something to do, and gave him an update on her Mexican house.

After a few more minutes of getting caught up, they agreed to get together, even just for coffee, though his new job would make it more difficult to do. They'd nevertheless keep in touch.

Chapter Twenty-One

Arriving at home after his first day at his new job, Brad was glad to see it was a good time to phone Meagan who should be home from work. He was about to call her when his phone rang. He picked it up and had the sheer pleasure of hearing her cheery voice, "Hi, darling. How was your first day at work?"

"I was just going to call *you*," Brad replied.

"I just got home and wanted to hear about your first day."

"Thanks, sweetheart. I very much enjoyed my day as a columnist for The Coast Journal. The column will be called Coastal Business and be headed up with my mugshot."

"It sounds exciting. I'll look forward to the first edition. I might even cut out your photo and pin it on my wall. Then I can show everyone my favorite journalist."

"Let's not get too far ahead of things," he

chuckled. "But I *will* look forward to interviewing you someday. I'll write something about Cindy's store and her remarkable associate Meagan Atherton, a big-city clothing and fashion mentor."

"I'm not sure she'd like me to be hogging the spotlight. I'll stand back and watch."

"We could come up with another word. Maybe something like—"

"I'll stay in the background until such time as I buy into the business. Then I'd expect you to write something wonderfully positive and attention-getting."

"Consider it done. By the way, I talked to Alexis today. She's feeling restless and concerned about her Mexican house."

"I know she gets anxious about it."

Their conversation ended with him telling about a District of Sechelt interview he did regarding upgrades to the aquatic center. Neither he nor

Meagan had yet used the facility. They agreed to go swimming someday soon. At least check it out.

Brad's first week at the Journal went smoothly. He interviewed some agreeable and interesting business owners; still others, he almost had to coax information out of them. Granted, they may have been busy, and he did sometimes have to wait to get what he needed. He wanted to interview as many business people – owners and managers – as quickly as possible. By the end of the week, he had some good material to include in his first column at the end of the following week. A couple of his Emma-directed business features would be published at the same time. As far as his time management was concerned, not having to work from the office was a big bonus. He could get more work done, and the week had gone by in a blur.

He and Meagan communicated every day and often shared dinners. He always enjoyed her positive take on things. She inspired him. He especially looked forward to the time they spent together on weekends. She'd be having dinner at his place on the following Sunday, preceded by an afternoon hike in Sechelt's Kinnikinnick Park.

On a cool Wednesday evening in early September, Brad and Chris sat on the Lighthouse deck overlooking Porpoise Bay, a favored spot even at that time of year. They placed their drink orders: Okanagan Pale Ale and Heineken. Chris had for years enjoyed Heineken ever since he and a friend enjoyed visitor time in the Amsterdam brewery's social room drinking free beer — a courtesy given especially to tourists.

Chris opened the conversation with pent-up curiosity. "The other night, you said you've been calling on businesses on Cowrie Street. Did you, by any chance, go into Pepe's Pizza?"

"Not yet. Why do you ask?" Brad said.

"There's a cashier there named Nicki. A tall girl with long brown hair and big eyes, very attractive.

And she's new in town. I had a pizza there the other day, and she's great to talk to. I'd like to get to know her and see if there's any hope of taking her out. She's probably in her thirties and isn't wearing any rings. I've been there a couple of times. She's nice, but there hasn't been time to really say much to her. It's hard to say much when she's busy serving customers."

"You might have to get to know her with your own creativity," Brad suggested. "Try some light-hearted banter and even some teasing if you think you could pull it off."

"The problem is I don't have your kind of confidence when it comes to meeting women."

"Take your time and do little things that show you're interested, like a compliment about something. Then, if she does little extras for you, she might be showing she's interested as well. And if you can do something to help her, that's even better … you know, pick something up or wipe spilled coffee on the counter."

Chris smiled and said, “You make it sound so easy. I’ll give it a try. But I don’t want to——“

The server approached and placed their drinks on the table.

Brad raised his glass. “Chris, here’s to your successful foray in getting to know Nicki.”

“Gee, thanks. By the way, when I first hiked with you, you mentioned a girlfriend in Vancouver. What happened in that situation?”

Brad told how they couldn’t stay together because they wanted completely different lifestyles.

“Were you living together?”

He shook his head. “No, we were both high octane, almost too busy and independent. How about you? How long were you married?”

“I started late at age thirty-five and had been married for nine years before getting divorced last year. It ended because she had begun a cozy relationship with one of my neighbors. Thankfully, we had no children. But Brad, if you're looking for your ideal lifestyle, what about Meagan?"

Brad put down his glass. "I was hoping to meet the woman of my dreams and, thank goodness, I met Meagan, who has made me rethink what is most important in a relationship. I now believe what a poet once wrote, that a couple's love should be like a song sung harmoniously from the same sheet of music."

"Both people have to do it," Chris said. "And I know the outcome firsthand when they don't."

"Meagan has made me feel we're in it for the long haul, and I've felt it more strongly every day. We're on the same page."

"You're beginning to sound poetic," Chris said. "But couldn't you and your Vancouver girlfriend have figured something out?"

"I'll just say that we had completely different thoughts about what we wanted in life."

Their server returned; they each ordered

another drink and placed their orders. Over dinner, their conversation turned from personal to general. At one point, Chris scanned the deck and said, “There’s a guy sitting at a table near the railing who was such a pest to one of my female hikers on the trail that I told him if he didn’t stop it, he couldn’t hike with us again. In fact, he’s the same guy I heard talking about Meagan. I told you about it.”

Looking in the direction Chris indicated, Brad saw Will Hackett and another man sitting at a table. Will looked at Brad with the same arrogant smirk as usual.

“Chris, I’m not surprised to see him here. In fact, I anticipated it happening one day.”

“You know this guy?”

“Only by chance. He was at Meagan’s the day I helped out. He seems to be a friend of Meagan’s sister Alexis. They had to kick him out one evening when he showed up with a bottle of rum while the girls were enjoying dinner and a movie. He lives nearby. Too close for Meagan's comfort."

Chris shook his head. "Wow, that's not good."

"I agree, but I think part of his problem is that he's very immature, like some dumb-ass college kid who sees everything in a gee-whiz kind of way when he's out and about."

"You're being very generous. He sounds like the type who will eventually end up doing something really stupid." Brad nodded.

After dinner, each man ordered a coffee and his favorite liqueur: Brad liked Kahlua, and Chris had Baileys Irish Cream. While they were enjoying their coffees, Will and his companion began leaving. As Will passed their table, he bumped into it, spilling some of the coffee and drinks. An accident or—?

He stopped. "Oops, sorry, did I do that?" he said, squinting.

Brad quickly stood up, pressed his hand on Will's shoulder and said," If you're too drunk to walk straight, you should leave."

"I'm not going anywhere," Will said.

"Well, maybe you should," Brad looked at the other fellow. "I hope you're the one driving."

The commotion soon reached the ears of management, and Will, obviously having had too much to drink, was asked to leave the building. Their attractive young server cleaned up the table and asked them if they'd like a refill, including a complimentary liqueur, an offer not to refuse.

"Nice going being so patient with him," Chris said.

"If he tried to punch me, I'd simply block it. He wasn't much to be concerned about. He looked pretty unsteady. It might've been an accident. Besides, why get messy and build bigger problems? It's a small town, and I'm still surprised at how often you can interact with the same people on a single day. The driver you gave the finger to today could be the one who is preparing your restaurant dinner tonight, and you wouldn't want to find something nasty in your soup."

Chris laughed, and they soon changed the subject. Brad told about a TV program he had seen showing a veterinarian removing a plastic toy from a dog's stomach.

He looked at Chris quizzically. "How often would *you* have to do something like that? It looked so invasive it's surprising the animal can recover. But it walked around the next day, seemingly none the worse."

"We do it fairly often. It's like a small child ingesting things that need to be taken out. But animals tend to have a better time of it, with much less stress."

"I'd expect that much of what you do for animals you could do for humans, too. For instance, if I needed stitches or a broken bone reset, you could do that for me, right?" And not just injuries, but also some regular maintenance."

Chris nodded enthusiastically. "Absolutely, all kinds of things. For instance, on Thursday, I'm having a neutering special."

Brad chuckled. "I'll keep it in mind."

Later, as he drove home, he thought about Meagan; he looked forward to having her at his place on Sunday for dinner. Tomorrow, he'd think about what to prepare for dinner to make it special. Lobster would be perfect.

He turned onto Marine Drive, scanning his rearview mirror, at the same time thinking, *"He wouldn't be that stupid … or would he?"*

Chapter Twenty-Two

Saturday dawned darkly, with wind-driven rain beating on Brad's bedroom windows. He had to get up and get things done, but the fury outside only encouraged him to get deeper under the covers. As he lay there, he heard a Harbour Air float plane taking off just as they did every day, rain or shine, transporting passengers. He got up, made coffee and, wanting to know more about the Beaver, went to his computer.

He learned that since the first DHC-2 Beaver rolled off the de Havilland production line in Toronto on Aug. 16, 1947, it had been revered by pilots worldwide for its dependability in transporting passengers and materials of all kinds. As a float-equipped bush plane, it helped open up Canada's north. In the early fifties, during the Korean War, it transported troops and supplies. And today, in many countries around the world – especially in Canada and the United States – whether on wheels or floats, the Beaver continues to provide dependable service. Brad thought he'd someday book a flight to Vancouver for him and Meagan. With the float-plane base being so close, it couldn't be handier.

Today, there were things to do at home: three loads of laundry as well as some vacuuming. The following day being Sunday, he wanted to be free of chores so he could hike with Meagan before preparing their dinner. All morning, he rethought about what to serve, everything from steaks to seafood. He preferred seafood, and, knowing Meagan's food preferences, he surmised she would too. Returning to his original thought about lobster, he phoned the fish market and learned they had sold their last whole lobster, but they did have frozen lobster tails. He asked that four be saved; he'd call for them in mid-afternoon.

After finishing household chores and having lunch, he went to The Brew House, where he enjoyed his usual espresso coffee and Adel's good-natured repartee. They had their usual lively banter, reminding him of how pleasant she was. After talking with her, he could see she might be a bit older than he originally thought, perhaps mid-thirties. He should talk to Chris about her. He was about mid-forties, and they'd have about the same age difference as between Brad and Meagan. A perfectly normal number of years difference in male-female relationships. He finished his coffee, thinking he'd give Chris a heads-up tomorrow.

Later, he shopped for the items he needed for dinner. Dessert would be whichever struck him as being the perfect one to compliment the main course. He might choose chocolate cheesecake, something that would satisfy Meagan's and his chocolate liking. At the fish market, he picked up his lobster tails.

"Good thing you asked us to hold them for you," said a tall, bearded man behind the counter. "Saturday's always busy. They can go pretty fast."

His last call was to the liquor store for some

Okanagan Sauvignon Blanc wine. He liked knowing that it had been made by British Columbia vintners who routinely win awards for VQA (Vintners Quality Alliance) quality. The province's Okanagan region had, within thirty years, become one of Canada's premier wine-producing regions, its vintners equaling and even surpassing the quality of many long-established Ontario wine producers. They were also giving America's Napa Valley and a range of European vintners some sharp competition.

Back at home, he thought about phoning Meagan, but she'd still be at work. He knew she and Alexis were going to go out for dinner that night, and he mightn't have an opportunity to speak to her. He decided to wait and phone her in the morning. Then he set the lobster tails out to thaw. He always looked forward to dinner preparations for guests, now especially for the woman he loved. It had to be perfect.

Sunday dawned sunny and calm, a perfect day

for hiking. Nighttime's chill had been dispersed by the sun's rays when only a hand breadth above the horizon. It'd be a matchless day for a pleasant hike with Meagan in a magnificent rainforest and the pleasure of her company at dinner.

Shortly after ten o'clock, he phoned her. "Hi Brad, you caught me drying dishes. When the phone rang, I hoped I'd hear your voice."

"Good morning, my dear. Are you all set for hiking, Kinnikinnick?"

"I'm *so* looking forward to it. But I'm in a bit of a quandary as to what to wear. I don't want to be dressed like a hiker when at your place for dinner. I'd like to look more elegant than that. Can you see me sitting down to dinner with blue jeans and boots?" she said before adding, "I'll, of course, bring a change of clothes, something new. I think you'll like it."

"But Meagan, we aren't going to be slugging through a quagmire. We'll be on well-maintained paths, and even the brambles are well away from the trail. The only things we have to be concerned about are cougars and the odd grizzly bear." He chuckled.

"I know they show up in certain areas from time to time, and from what I hear about Kinnikinnick, it's well away from their usual haunts. But if we do see them, I know you'll protect me."

"I will, my darling. Together to the end."

Later, at her place, they were quickly in each other's arms. They gazed into each other's eyes and kissed lovingly before Brad suggested that they get going.

"Today, I'm taking my camera," he said. "In my enthusiasm to get on the trail, I often forget about photos, but I'm taking some today, and you will have the starring role."

"Am I dressed alright?" she said. She was wearing tan-colored slacks, a matching jacket and good running shoes.

"You look great and ready for the trail."

When they arrived at Kinnikinnick several other cars were there, not surprising on such a perfect day. Brad parked and led Meagan to the trail head.

She stood looking in wonderment. "This truly is a beautiful place. I don't know why I haven't taken the time to check it out."

He took her by the hand. "I discovered it for the first time when I came here with the hiking group. Look at how the high canopy forms a kind of leafed dome overhead with such surreal grandeur. I call it Mother Nature's cathedral because when you step in under the high canopy, that's what it's like. It's no wonder people will hug such majestic and imposing trees. This one (pointing) has a trunk diameter of about five feet, is more than one hundred feet high and is hundreds of years old. Thank goodness they left it alone. Stand beside it, Meagan, and I'll take a photo."

Farther along, he took another photo, this one

with her standing on a wooden walkway crossing a small stream. The trails were like others in the local parks that were typically maintained by the Rotary or Lions clubs. Lining the trails were various kinds of endemic and ancient varieties of plants, some of them used for centuries by original peoples for food and medicine. Some plants are known to be toxic, even poisonous, especially some unfamiliar mushrooms. In addition to the variety of vegetation, small animals – squirrels, chipmunks and birds – could often be seen in the trees and underbrush.

As they walked along the trail, two things stood out in Brad's mind: the environment's soul-soothing tranquility and beauty and the pleasure of sharing it with Meagan. It warmed his heart to see her on the path and know she was there because he was there. It was a case of being part of each other's life and fully enjoying it.

After the hike and returning to Brad's house, Meagan tidied up before going to the kitchen, where she found him looking in the fridge.

"You still haven't told me what you're making for dinner," she said. "Is it a secret?"

He looked up. "Not really … more of a surprise."

"Can't you tell me what it is?"

"It's something that lives in the sea."

She put her hand to her face. "Brad, what *is* it?"

"It's lobster tail, something I thought would be a nice treat."

"Sweetheart, I can't eat shellfish."

"Like lobster?"

"Yes, lobster as well as shrimp and crab. I'm sorry, I wish you had told me. It's not your fault. We're still finding things out."

"Believe it or not, as I laid in bed this morning thinking about meal preparation, I thought about the fact that many people are allergic to shellfish and hoped you weren't. Then I thought if you were, we'd go to Plan B and have dinner at the pub."

"What will happen to the lobster tails?"

"I'll leave them in the fridge and cook them tomorrow after work, and then microwave them for other meals, which will be handy during my work week."

She put her arm around him. "Let's not go out for dinner. I'd rather have an intimate dinner here with you and wear my new outfit. Why not get two dinners for take-out? We can prepare whatever goes with it, salad or whatever."

He thought for a moment. "I already have the dessert. Let's do it. We've got lots of time to relax, have a glass of wine and decide what we want for dinner."

He put on some music, and they sat enjoying wine and roasted cashews, her favorite. At one point, she took his hand and leaned into him. "You keep surprising me with your being so unflappable about things."

"What kinds of things?"

"Changeups, your Plan B for needs of the moment. Some people get flustered having their plans reduced or changed. You patiently go with the flow and are open to logical solutions."

He nodded thoughtfully. "Well, I ran the kind of business that had to have something on the pages. If one of the pieces wasn't ready for publishing, there had better be another to fill in for it, and it had better look seamless."

She kissed his neck, saying, "I like seamless."

He gazed at her and raised his brow suggestively, "Such a seamless time before dinner?"

She smiled, nodded and hand-in-hand, they went upstairs.

Later, while contentedly lying together, Brad said, "I love you so much, Meagan. We were made for each other and must have met and loved in another life."

"It's as if we've discovered each other again."

He gently kissed her lips and ran his hand over the smooth curve of her shoulder. "Your skin is so smooth it's a treat to touch you."

"And I *love* your touch. Sometimes, when you look at me, I wish your eyes were your hands."

"You might not think that if I couldn't keep my hands off you. There are men like that, always groping."

She gave him a quick kiss, swung her legs off the bed and said, "Well, thank goodness you're not one of them."

He grinned. "Let's head for the shower."

"You go first. Then you can get dressed and pick up the dinners. It'll give me time to shower and fix my makeup. You don't want to look across the table at a woman with smeared makeup, do you?"

He laughed. “Hell, yes.”

Later, as she came down the stairs dressed in her dinner clothes, a chartreuse-print wrap dress, he stood watching her descend and thinking he had never seen her look more alluring. As she stepped down, he lightly pulled her into his arms, murmuring, “You look ravishing, and I’m so glad we’re staying in.” Kissing her, he added, “Now I've got to go and pick up our dinners.”

While she got ready, he went online and checked the Buccaneer’s menu. He called the restaurant and ordered two meals for pickup: roasted chicken breast and sockeye salmon, knowing she enjoyed salmon. Both meals with trimmings. No desserts. He was told the kitchen wasn’t especially busy and he could pick them up in about twenty minutes.

After picking up the meals, he put them in the microwave for a quick warmup and then put them onto plates. Meagan then put the salad into bowls, and they were soon sitting at the table with the dinner in front of them. He poured their wine and, raising his glass, toasted the chef, whoever he or she was.

“I could have been toasting you,” Meagan said. “I’m sorry.”

“Don’t be sorry. My fault, not yours.”

When they had finished their entrees, he said, “Dessert is a surprise I know you won’t have any problem with.” He walked to the kitchen and returned with a covered ceramic plate.

He reached for the lid. “Any guesses?”

She peered at it, looking for a hint, and seeing nothing, said, “Chocolate cheesecake?”

With that, he laughed and raised the lid with a flourish. “It was a no-brainer being something we both like – a lot. You can take half of it home.”

“I’ll take a couple of pieces to work with me. Cindy will like it, too.”

Later, while they were enjoying tea, she lightly

massaged her thigh.

"How are you feeling after the hike? Any aches?"

She shook her head. "No, nothing serious. A bit of stiffness that more hikes and stretching should fix. And you? I heard you stumble on some high roots. I wasn't taking any chances with them and stepped high."

"Some trails have really high ones like those today, and they *can* trip people quite often. I usually step high, too, but I was distracted today."

"Are you talking about me?"

He chuckled and walked to his stereo. "Let's dance."

They smoothly danced through a variety of selections until his thoughts about having to start work in the morning moved him to say, "Meagan, I hate to say this, but I have to attend a meeting first thing in the morning, and I've got to be sharp."

"It's been on my mind, too, and here we are

dancing the light fantastic. It's been a wonderful day that must sadly end, and I'm missing you already."

"Well, my dear, the wonderful thing about living in Sechelt is that we're never far away. Five minutes max."

As he drove her home, they talked about their jobs, and by eleven-thirty, both were in their beds. The coming week had been on his mind all weekend, and that night, he reveled in the thought of seeing his first column, an accumulation of his first two weeks of interviews.

Before Meagan fell asleep, she heard an unusual sound outside her window. Like other times, it defined nothing in particular, certainly nothing aggressive or dangerous. It sounded different, like a light thud. Even though worrisome, she wouldn't call Brad for another useless drive-over. She'd try to forget about it unless something *really* startled her, at which point she'd call him. It made her think about her love for him and his love for her. Not having Brad in her life had become unthinkable.

Chapter Twenty-Three

On Monday morning, Brad again saw how Emma was a guiding light. After the regular meeting, she asked Brad to meet her in her office when he had a minute. She suggested that he first get himself a cup of coffee. Returning with his coffee and seeing her empty cup, he said, “Emma, I should have asked you if you wanted one, too.”

“Thanks, Brad. I’ve already had a couple at home. I try to limit it to three or four cups a day, but it sometimes goes higher, the convenience of having it on hand.”

“An omnipresent lure,” Brad suggested.

Emma smiled. “Indeed.”

She shuffled some papers on her desk, found what she was looking for and, reading from one of them, said, “You may haven’t heard of a company called Benno Builders. They’ve been contracted by the District of Sechelt to do renovations to some of the district offices. I'd like a feature story about the company by Wednesday. No more than about twelve-hundred words. I'll give you this (handing him a sheet of paper) that has background information and contacts. Now, I want to tell you that our publisher, Mr. Harrison, won't be coming back to work for a while. He's beginning rounds of chemotherapy. I mentioned his cancer to you some time back. So until he returns, I'll be editor and general manager. Needless to say, I have my fingers crossed that everything will turn out alright."

"I didn't realize things were that serious."

Emma nodded. "They are at the moment. I'll keep you posted."

"With you at the helm, I'm sure things will go well. But if you ever suddenly need extra help, let me know."

"Thanks, Brad. I appreciate it."

As Brad was leaving and passing the coffee

nook, he heard conversation and laughter. He took the opportunity to stop and have some quick interaction with the staff: Ellen, a cute, young redhead in advertising; Clarence, a forty-something joker in the same department; Mildred, a pleasant middle-aged woman in accounting; Evan, a mustachioed thirty-something writer; another writer, Lloyd, a plump, fiftyish man with whom he had previously chatted with in the coffee nook. They were a friendly and agreeable bunch. He looked forward to getting to know them better as time went on. He went to his desk, phoned Benno Builders and secured an appointment with the president of the company for two o'clock the following day. He then made a list of calls for his column. Some of them he'd call upon, others he'd handle with a phone call.

At day's end, he felt he had achieved some good interviews, with useful inroads made to others. As he drove home, feeling buoyed, he thought about stopping at the Megalos' for a quick visit. Pulling up in front of the house, he could see Eric in the shed cutting something on a bench with a handheld electric saw. Seeing Brad, Eric shouted, “Yasou, it’s about time you dropped by.”

“I wanted to see you and Connie and, of course, see how your finger’s doing. I wasn’t far away, and I thought I’d take the opportunity to stop by. But I don’t want to take up your time.”

“What time? If I don’t work this time, I’ll make up for it another time. I'm the boss, not time. Of course, time can sometimes bite my ass, but not today. I’ll set this down and we can go in the house and have a drink. It’s *that* time. The sun’s a long way past the yardarm.”

“What time of the day does that refer to?”

“It means it’s time for the ship’s officers to have a morning drink at eleven o’clock. At least in our part of the world, the sun will show above the yardarm, the top horizontal bar, at that time of the morning. They called it “stand easy” time. Not bad working conditions, eh?"

Brad said, "I know it's common usage that five o'clock in the afternoon is time to have a drink, at least here."

"That's dinner time, when the officers next imbibe – a lot – yardarm or no yardarm. Let's go in the house. Connie will be glad to see you."

When he had put things away, Eric held up his left hand and wiggled what was left of the finger. "It doesn't look bad, does it? And it works great."

Brad agreed, saying, "It just looks like a littler little finger."

"Littler little finger," Eric chuckled as he closed the shop door. "The good thing is it isn't slowing me down one bit."

They walked into the house. "Connie, look who's here."

"I saw you drive up. How are you, Brad?" she said from the kitchen.

“I've been busy with the Journal, of course, but there always seems to be something else that pops up to keep things on the back burner. I’m sorry for not getting in touch sooner.”

Eric went to the kitchen and returned with a bottle of ouzo, two small glasses (Connie demurred) and a cream pitcher of water, after which they all sat down. “The important thing is you’re here, and we’re glad to see you. We can relax and get caught up on things since we last saw you. How’s that beautiful woman of yours … Meagan, right?”

“Yes, Meagan. We’re seeing more of each other, as well as her sister, Alexis, and that keeps us busier. And with my job at the paper, the days fly by.”

“Time has a way of challenging us,” said Eric. “But we have to remember *we’re* the time keeper.”

Brad nodded and bent to see Eric’s hand. “What surprises me is how cleanly it has healed. It’s not at all looking like one that has survived such an extreme injury.”

"The doctors told me because the finger had been pulled into the saw so quickly, it cut off cleanly with none of the collateral damage that is so often the case. I researched finger replacement on Google, and some of the fingers were in horrible condition, even after the procedure. Yes, I feel lucky."

Connie placed her hand on Eric's shoulder. "He never complains. There is a certain amount of nerve damage that sometimes exerts itself, like the other night in bed when I felt his hand twitching on my backside and——"

Eric laughed. "It wasn't what you'd think. It really was nerve spasms that sometimes occurred even at night when I was sleeping. But it got Connie's attention real quick."

Brad laughed. "I know that certain kinds of nerve pain can do that. I've experienced it myself."

Eric said, "You're seeing more of Meagan. She's a lovely woman, and I hope you two stay together. She's a keeper."

Connie agreed that Meagan was the right kind of woman for Brad.

"You're similar in many ways and so compatible. She's prettier, though (she laughed), but you're a close second. You look like you were meant for each other."

"We know we have something to hold onto and build on," Brad said, "And every day, I'm reminded how lucky I am to have her in my life."

Eric nodded thoughtfully. "Just be careful of strong currents that can pull you away from shore and happiness."

Brad grinned. "I couldn't have said it better."

Connie looked at Eric. "Do you remember our Toronto neighbor Floyd Felden and his girlfriend Heather? Remember how she told him she wasn't going to wait around forever."

Eric laughed. "And she didn't."

"I know it happens, and it's not something we

want to put off. We're doing a lot of planning, as you'll see before long. Lots of things to consider," Brad said as he glanced at the wall clock. "But I see it's getting on, so I'd best be going."

Connie looked at him searchingly. "Can't you stay for dinner?"

"Thanks, Connie, but I have to get some things done. And I want to have the two of you to my place for dinner as soon as I get my work routine better established."

Brad went to his car and drove away, waving at Eric and Connie, who stood at their door waving back. As he turned onto the road, he scanned his rearview mirror as always. *So far, so good.*

Shortly after arriving at home he received a message from Karen.

Hi Brad –

I thought I'd contact you after having a couple of thoughts today. When you and I broke up, we remained friends, and I feel it left an opening for me to send this note today. Nothing serious, just a thought that we were both idealistic and ideals often aren't realistic. My thought today is, if our ideals have changed, would it make any difference?

Basically, what I'm saying is that we don't know how things will go in the future, and if one of us has an abrupt change of thought, I think it should be communicated to the other – at least in the near future.

Please see it as an open and constructive concept that many people would have wished for in their own breakups. Time cancels many opportunities to discuss and reshape things. I'd be pleased to hear from you if ever you feel there's anything we should talk about.

I hope you are happy and well.

Love, Karen

Brad gazed at the message that invited

consideration for contact should he ever wish to discuss “things.” Brad admired her for that, but their relationship had become well untied. There would be no going back to old love and the cloudiness of conflicting ideals. In Brad’s new life, the sunshine shone brighter. He went to the kitchen and had a drink of water before replying.

Hi Karen:

Thanks for the well-said message that I respect for its openness. I agree that because we didn’t part in bad faith, we should be able to send a message that invites thinking about how things happen and how they could be reshaped if – But the ifs aren’t part of the equation in my new world because I’m involved with a woman who is on the same page as me. We want the same things. It’s a lucky thing for people, especially of our age, to find each other so mutually compatible in the things we want from life. There’s not much else to say except thanks for your considerate message.

I hope all goes well with you, as I'm sure it will.

Brad

In the morning, Brad put some finishing touches to the day's work plan. His primary appointment was the two o'clock interview with Benno Builder's president, T.J. Ogilvie. When Brad arrived at the office he was struck by the interior's ambience that said volumes about how the company could turn wood and metal into spectacular spaces. Exotic woods and stainless steel were tasteful highlights, with furniture to match everything of uncommon quality. Even the receptionist took the cake for looks. Her auburn hair and cut pageboy style framed her attractive features. Her dress looked like it might've come from an upscale Vancouver store.

She was further enhanced by her classy demeanor. Brad was quickly ushered into Mr. Ogilvie's office and, to his astonishment, was met by a large, neatly-bearded man who wore slacks with mud on one of the knees. He explained that he had just returned from a building site that had sudden and unexplained water seepage. He obviously typified a leader who would go into the trenches to solve a problem. He came to their meeting obviously feeling stressed, *'I have to apologize because I don't have a lot of time today'*, so he sat for a somewhat hurried interview. He then arranged for the receptionist to send several interior and exterior photos of recent office renos the company had completed.

The interview hadn't gone exactly as expected, a reminder that everyone has their own timeline and activities to factor into what is wanted of their time. There can often be call backs. In this case, Brad arranged for another appointment for a photo, one that would be done with sensitivity. With the camera pointed, there's nothing worse than seeing a busy person sitting behind a desk looking harried or glum. Brad always liked to make them smile because, as he said, "They'll be happier when they see the result."

The rest of the day went smoothly, something

more easily accomplished in a small town, especially one with abundant retail businesses. At the office, he dropped by Clarence's desk to discuss potential leads from Brad's business column and Clarence's advertising that could be beneficial to both of them. Clarence chuckled and said, "Back scratchers. Sounds good."

On Friday morning, Brad's first column appeared. Mr. Ogilvie sent an email to Emma saying how pleased he was with it. She passed it onto Brad with her own accolades. Brad also enjoyed the heartfelt phone call he received from Meagan.

"Good morning, sweetheart. Cindy and I both enjoyed your column. Lots of info and well written. I think you deserve some special care. How about dinner at my place tonight?"

"I couldn't imagine anything better, my darling. What time?"

"Cindy wouldn't mind if I left a bit early. How about six thirty? I'm looking forward to seeing you."

When their conversation ended, Brad sat at his desk, finishing some paperwork. He was about to leave the office when Emma approached.

"Brad, I want to say again how pleased I am with your column. I've received phone calls and emails from a variety of people and businesses who are pleased to see another kind of focus in the Journal. Of course, many of them are expecting you to write them up, so I'll give you some more names to contact when you feel they're appropriate for a particular column. And, as you know, your Benno feature got good comments from Mr. Ogilvie. So again, good job."

Brad arrived home with little more than an hour to spare before going to Meagan's house. He had a quick shower and sat on the sofa to relax for a while. As he casually looked around him, his eyes fell upon his photo albums. Thanks to photo-taking help from another hiker, there were a couple of photos of him and Meagan standing together beside a very large tree. Then there were the photos of Meagan he had taken himself. It pleased him to know that he could enjoy more photos of her.

Chapter Twenty-Four

When Brad walked into Meagan's house, he quickly found himself in a warm embrace. "I'm so glad to see you," she enthused, holding him close.

Brad kissed her and kissed her again. "Thanks for your wonderful invitation. It's exactly what I needed."

Meagan gazed at him lovingly. "It's what I needed, too. The week seemed to go on forever. Now that you're working, it takes up so much more of your time, and it makes me realize how my work does the same."

"It means we'll have to be more creative, more spontaneous about how and when we see each other," he suggested. "We'll set up schedules to create new energies as in the first law of thermodynamics."

She raised an eyebrow. "I think you're going a bit too far. Do you know the first law of thermodynamics?"

He grinned. "Energy cannot be created or destroyed. It can only be transformed. In our case, transformed into new things to do."

"Alright, smarty pants, but in the first law of kitchen dynamics, I've transformed some very disparate items into something completely different. You'll see, but first, there's time to relax for a while."

In the living room, they sat enjoying wine and some favorite music as they got caught up on the week's happenings. She congratulated him once again on his column and business features, telling him how proud she was of his successful passage into the world of newspaper journalism. She knew he'd do well and assured him she'd in no way resent his time away from her when things got busier. "The better one is at something, the busier they can become."

She had a sip of wine, put down her glass and looked at him. "I wasn't going to mention this and cause any needless worry about it. It's probably explainable."

"What is it?"

"A couple of nights ago, at around eleven-thirty like the last time, I had just gone to bed when I heard a slight thump on the side of the house near my bedroom window. Then, as I listened, I heard something brush against the wall. So I coughed to make it sound like I was awake and aware in case of it being a burglar. Then, it became quiet. I've always wondered if it's raccoons foraging. There's lots of them around here."

"Did it sound like it did the first time you called me?"

"I'm not sure. I've heard similar sounds before and didn't call you because it wasn't really loud or aggressive."

He shook his head. "You should still let me know when it happens. I want to see if I can find out what it is. Haven't they *all* been at about the same time, just before midnight?"

She thought for a moment. "I think so. But couldn't some of it be raccoons? They're everywhere."

"I suppose it could be. It's a good thing you have screens on the windows. I've seen television episodes showing city raccoons climbing almost anywhere in and on buildings. And they don't like people intervening. They can actually be quite hissy and aggressive."

Meagan put her hand on Brad's knee. "Well, enough of that. I haven't told you what we're having for dinner. I know you'll like it. Can you guess what it is?"

"Stew?"

"No, it's beef lasagna. You once told me you sometimes buy various kinds of frozen lasagna dinners to heat up because they're handy. So I made lots, and you can take some home."

As they listened to the music, he couldn't help thinking. *It doesn't seem logical or possible, but it could be him. It's time to make some security improvements.*

Meagan continued, "It's a pretty standard lasagna, basically consisting of lasagna noodles, ground beef and pasta sauces, cottage cheese, parsley, parmesan cheese, as well as mozzarella cheese."

"It sounds delicious. It also sounds like a lot of work."

"In my laboratory, transformations can be made quickly," she said, squeezing his knee. "Oh, and I've got cherry and walnut squares for dessert."

They continued rehashing the day's events and the shape of his work-a-day world until other happenings worked their way into the discussion.

"I saw Alexis yesterday," Meagan said. "She

dropped by to say hi and tell me the latest. I don't know why, but she had Will over to her place recently about a possible fix-up for her car. As you know, Will has told her he'd be happy to help if it became necessary. And she seemed very comfortable with it."

Brad tilted his head. "Could there be something going on we don't know or suspect, such as a budding romance?"

She grimaced. "Or a budding fling, something to help the time go by if she's really lonely, which I think she is. But as much as I love her, I can't see her every day."

He had a sip of wine. "I guess if one *is* lonely enough, Will can do for the company. But in fairness to him, he's not a bad-looking guy, and he likes to be helpful. It's just his childish attitude that needs getting used to. He often says things not only before he thinks, but they're often way out in left field, total non-sequiturs."

"I think that's because he is not very confident, especially around women. I noticed when painting at my place that he tries too hard to be in the conversation, whether he has something significant to say or not."

Brad nodded knowingly. "It reminds me of a Plato quote about that sort of thing, *'Wise men talk because they have something to say; fools because they have to say something.'*

"But I think he also has a shy side that he tries to cover up with bravado."

"But I can't imagine Alexis putting up with it. Although I can see her having a calming effect on him, she is generally calm and confident."

Meagan said, "By the way, I smell the lasagna."

She dashed to the kitchen; dinner was almost ready. Brad, as usual, liked to help out, and he did some slicing of a small Italian loaf before pouring wine. They sat on opposite sides of the table, its small size giving them heightened feelings of togetherness. After a couple of mouthfuls, he reached and squeezed her hand. “The best lasagna I've ever tasted.”

Later, they sat on the sofa with cups of tea – Meagan had refused to think about doing dishes – while soft music surrounded them in a melodic enhancement of their togetherness.

Inspired by the music, Brad took her by the hand and, before dancing, looked deeply into her eyes and held her in a total-body embrace, wanting to inhale every bit of her essence. He kissed her cheeks, and his mouth lingered on hers to feel the warmth and fullness of her lips that intoxicated him and sometimes weakened his knees, she being the only woman who ever made it happen.

They danced in perfect synchronicity, each step as if they had been wired to do it. And just as they were wired to dance, so too were they wired to love with the same mind. As they danced, it became impossible to continue without yielding to the maddening excitation of their closeness.

The music played on as they stood in the middle of the room in a passionate embrace as Brad hotly kissed her. Then, taking his hand, she led him to the bedroom, where they were soon lost in their special world, a seemingly infinite universe, after which they'd return to their other world. In both worlds, their love was undeniable.

The following morning, though it was Saturday, Meagan had to go to work. Brad would go home, have a shower, and have some lasagna for breakfast. He'd eat the rest of it for lunch or dinner. Before they separated at the door, she reminded him that she had been invited to Alexis' place for dinner. She wanted to show Meagan things she wished to give away before going to Mexico. He had, of course, been invited, but he declined, wanting a quiet night so he could do some work and the sisters could enjoy some time together.

On Saturday morning, Meagan and Cindy had their usual coffee and some girl talk before opening the store. The first thing Cindy said to Meagan was a shocker. “After you left last night, a man called and asked for you. He seemed confused when asking for you. He also asked about Brad.”

“What did you tell him?”

“I asked his name, and he muttered something about it being kind of personal and hung up. There was no phone number, probably a pay phone.”

Meagan felt alarmed. “I don’t know who it could be. I haven’t met any men socially since coming to Sechelt; no one, of course, except Brad. Then there’s Will. My gut instinct tells me it could only be someone from Vancouver, but I can’t imagine who. I knew many men in the clothing business, but none intimately. And I’m sure Adam wouldn’t be so sneaky and secretive. And craziest of all, asking about Brad.”

“He might call again today,” Cindy said. She added, “I’m sure there’ll be an easy explanation.”

After having coffee and a light breakfast, Brad decided his afternoon would include purchasing a dusk-to-dawn porch light for Meagan’s added security. Later, at lunch, he ate her lasagna and a chocolate chip muffin and thought about his evening being free. He had invited Meagan for Sunday dinner, so special preparations were needed. Tonight, he'd spiff things up for the occasion.

After lunch, as he was about to head downtown, he received a phone call from Meagan. “Hi Brad, are you busy?” There was tenseness in her voice.

“No, sweetheart, what’s happening?”

“I wasn’t going to phone you until later, but I want to try to solve a weird phone call that Cindy got at the shop last night after I left. Some guy phoned and asked about me. And he asked about you. He wouldn’t give his name or phone number and then hung up. Do you have any ideas about who that could be? I'm sure you don't, but I'm checking every angle."

"No, I'm drawing a blank on that. I can't imagine who it could be."

"It's kind of spooky the way he was so secretive. Cindy thinks he might call back today, so we'll see."

"I'm sure it's nothing serious, Meagan. Call me and let me know if he does call … or doesn't." "Will do. Bye, darling."

As he went over what she had told him, it made his blood run cold to think of Leonard Mason having any part in it. The chances of Mason doing it were slim, but you had to know him and his lack of control. Based on what Meagan had told him about Adam, he felt he might somehow be involved in the episodes, as foolish as they were. But what if the phone call led up to something worse, the other episodes being merely hints of greater mayhem by a fool like Mason?

It all underlined the need to pay more attention to Meagan's overall security. A dusk-to-dawn porch light would be a good start.

In Home Hardware, he found the style of light fixture he wanted. Later, he found her porch light unlit, suggesting the switch had been turned off. But maybe not. He did a simple test and tapped barbed wires to determine if the switch was on – it wasn't. He removed the somewhat rusted light fixture, attached the new one, and screwed in the sensor and bulb. Meagan would have to turn on the light switch and leave it on. The bulb wouldn't light up until dusk.

Meagan arrived home to be happily reminded of Brad's love and care. The new porch light looked magnificent – modern and attractive. In the house, she flipped the light switch on. The bulb didn't light up. She then wiggled the switch up and down, but the bulb still didn't light up. She thought it might be a bad connection or a faulty bulb. Brad would know.

He answered his phone and heard Meagan

say, “Can I speak to the electrician who installed my new porch light.”

“You’re talking to him.”

“Thank you so much, you thoughtful man. But I turned the light switch on, and it didn’t light up, so I’m wondering if the bulb is faulty.”

“Meagan, your bulb comes on only when it’s getting dark, and it turns off automatically with daylight. So you just leave the light switch on, and the bulb turns on and off by itself. I’m glad you like it; I’m going to install one here. I had one at my Vancouver house for years. Now tell me, were there any more mysterious phone calls.”

“No, and Cindy thinks it’s either a prank or some whacko who doesn’t know how to rein in his crazy ideas, and it probably won’t happen again.”

“Probably not, but I think you should be extra observant when you’re in and out of the house.”

“Brad, I appreciate your thoughts about

security, and I want you to know I feel secure just having you in my life.”

“Well, honey, I feel it the same way you do. I know you’d also give me the kind of backup I might need in various situations.”

She wholeheartedly agreed. “I think we’re a heroic partnership, dependable when the chips are down. I've known married couples who are exactly like that … Eric and Connie, for instance. And I think we’re like that.”

Brad nodded enthusiastically, “No doubt about it.”

Later, as he readied for bed, Brad thought about the times of night the sounds were heard near Meagan’s bedroom window, most often on a Saturday night at about eleven-thirty, but not always. He had a sudden inspiration: he'd go there tonight to see what he might find – what or who.

At eleven-thirty, he parked his car at the far end

of the block and walked to the rear of Ollie Sigurdson's house, where he stood hidden by bushes. He could see the back of Meagan's house but not the wall with her bedroom window. He moved to a small stand of trees and bushes that provided an oblique view of the wall and window. There, he waited. Moments later he thought he faintly heard something. He slowly turned, but too late. A dark figure had slipped away and ran to the highway to catch the midnight bus. It was someone who, only minutes before, had been standing near Meagan's bedroom window. An hour later, still seeing nothing, Brad drove home.

Chapter Twenty-Five

Several weeks had gone by since Brad and Chris last met at the pub. Most of Brad's time had been taken up by his day-to-day business activities and spending time with Meagan. Chris' days had been unusually busy and he'd made a couple of business trips to Vancouver. Now, it being a chilly, late-October night, they sat by a large window, the closest they'd get to their favorite place on the deck. They filled their time with conversations on a broad range of issues, from politics to the environment. The opposite sex never failed to be an interesting topic, especially for Chris, who didn't have a significant other in his life.

"You've had coffee at The Brew House. What do you think of Adel?" Brad said. "She seems to me like the kind of woman who could make any man happy."

"Yes, I like her. But she isn't really my type. I like the more studied kind of woman, the kind that you have to take time to get to really know, see what's in the deepest part of her mind. Call it being attracted to intellectual challenge or psychological gamesmanship, I suppose."

Brad chortled. "For all you know, what might be behind Adel's easygoing ways are intellectual leanings that might astound you."

"Did you see that in Meagan?"

Brad happily nodded. "That and *much* more."

Chris smiled. "Well, you've inspired me. Maybe I'll pop by Adel's and have coffee more often."

After more talk about singles' tactics and other issues – Brad's new job, Chris' operations on mainly cats and dogs – the evening ended on an optimistic note. Brad would look forward to knowing the outcome of Chris' venture.

Meagan and Alexis were going to the Spindrift Restaurant for dinner that evening. They both liked the restaurant's broad selection of seafood entrees. Alexis arrived at Meagan's house completely strung out.

“What have you got to offer your sister in the way of a drink? I need something to settle me down.”

Meagan looked askance. “What have you been up to that could cause you much stress?”

“My neighbor Elaine, you met her at my place once. She invited me to go with her to Gibsons to check out a new consignment store. She’s always looking for collectibles and certain kinds of clothes. And then she wanted to look at some specials at London Drugs. I like London Drugs, too, so I was happy to go with her. A big mistake. She checks everything, not just the items she’s looking for.”

Meagan stood with her hands on her hips. “I could give you a glass of white wine, and I have a bottle of tequila I bought because Brad likes it. You can have some if you think it’d help settle you down. I want us to have a pleasant and relaxing evening.”

“A glass of wine will be fine. And the way that woman drives is enough to get anyone stirred up. She drives way below the speed limit and frustrates drivers behind her. She brakes on every curve, no matter how sharp or broad it is. I didn’t think I’d ever get home in time to freshen up and change before picking you up for dinner. I've had to rush like mad. I hate being late. (she reached for the proffered drink) Thanks.”

“So, did you buy anything?”

“I bought some moisturizing cream and vitamin C. Elaine bought some lipstick, towels on special and a couple of other items. Nothing at the consignment store.”

“Did you notice anything different when you came to the door, the new porch light?”

Alexis had another sip of wine. “No, I didn’t.”

“Brad installed it while I was at work. It has a dusk-to-dawn bulb attachment that automatically turns the light on at night for added security.” Alexis nodded knowingly. “David and I had one at our house. I loved it. There’s never any darkness at the front door. How thoughtful of him."

Meagan poured herself a glass of wine and sat down. "One of the reasons he did it is because of something I haven't told you about. I've not only been hearing strange sounds by my house at night, but now a mysterious man phoned the store a couple of days ago asking about me. I had left the store, and when Cindy asked for his name and phone number, he hung up. There's been no call since. Needless to say, it spooked me a bit. And since then, I've been made to think about some of the things Adam said when I left him and got a divorce."

Alexis nodded knowingly. "I remember you telling me how he almost threatened you, something about you can't leave him. It's weird and makes no sense. Considering how meanly he treated you, *why* would you stay? Some men make threats when a woman dumps them. It's about their pride, their control over the relationship like she's a little girl who doesn't know what she's doing, 'She'll come back if I convince her she's making a mistake.'"

"I've heard of men trying to get back into a woman's life or clandestinely wanting to know what she's doing and with whom," Meagan said. "The last thing I want is to pit two men against each other. I know Brad would do whatever he thought necessary to protect me. Besides, I don't think Adam is that shallow or insecure. The only thing he ever did even close to those kinds of things was to drive by the home of a woman I was staying with when I shopped for a condo. One evening, he drove by as we sat on the front porch."

Alexis slowly shook her head. "It might be a good time to start being more alert to anything unusual going on. Do you ever have any of your neighbors walking through your property? Have you ever seen anything suspicious?"

"Not really. Why?"

"I wasn't going to say anything about it until I heard about the phone call. I had a chat with Will one day, and in the course of our conversation, he mentioned that he saw someone step behind your house one night when he drove by. Your car wasn't there."

"It could have been anyone."

"Well, because Will lives so close to you, I asked him to pay particular attention to what goes on around your property."

Meagan shook her head. "You didn't have to ask him to do that. In fact, Brad already did. I don't want *Will* to feel even the least responsible for my security or to drop by to see how I am."

"Even so, it'd be a simple matter for him to keep an eye out for snoopers." Alexis picked up her wine glass. "Let's finish our wine and go for dinner. I'm famished."

Sunday morning dawned crisp and bright, a perfect day for hiking or simply walking along the shore, the kind of day made for enthusiastic participation. Brad would be introducing Meagan to

Cliff Gilker Park, the scenic rainforest near Robert's Creek. It had been his favorite hike, and he looked forward to showing her its many features, such as well-maintained hiking trails, several waterfalls and a couple of creeks spanned by wooden bridges. Its abundant attractions made it a popular spot for families, hikers, photographers and nature lovers. As well as the forest's natural attractions, people also appreciated the large, grassed playing field, a children's playground and well-maintained public washrooms.

Brad made coffee and phoned Meagan. "Good morning, sunshine. We've got a perfect day for hitting the trails at Cliff Gilker Park."

"I'm *so* looking forward to it," she said enthusiastically. "What time do you want to start?"

"We've got lots of time. How about if I pick you up after lunch at, say, one-thirty?"

"That's good. It will give me time to get some things done around here."

"See you then, sweetheart."

He decided to do what had been put on the back burner too long. He phoned the Megalos' and invited them for dinner at his place; he suggested next Sunday. They happily thanked him for his invitation but said it'd have to be the following month. They were getting ready to go on a three-week trip to Greece, probably their last. Eric would call Brad when they returned. Brad wished them a safe and happy holiday, adding, "Have an ouzo for me."

He next made a catch-up call to his friend Jeffery. As a Vancouver radio sales rep, the station's newsroom routinely kept him abreast of city happenings.

"Jeff, I haven't heard anything about Mason. Have you heard any more news since his release or whereabouts?"

He *had* heard something, primarily that Mason had indeed been released a couple weeks ago but with no hint as to his whereabouts.

Chapter Twenty-Six

When Brad arrived at Meagan's house, he was surprised to see an unfamiliar car parked there. It quickly brought into focus his recent concerns about a stranger's intrusion into her privacy. She heard his car and opened her door, looking like a model for an outdoor/hiking magazine. She wore a colorful flannel shirt, black twill slacks, a sporty jacket and new Merrell hiking boots.

Brad raised his hands. "You look fantastic, very trail savvy."

"Brad, I want you to meet my friend Cindy. It's about time you two met."

Cindy had just arrived there, dressed for Sunday, not the trail. She wore navy-coloured slacks and an attractive, pale grey jacket with a matching scarf. She was tall, attractive and refreshingly friendly.

She held out her hand. "I'm glad to finally meet

you, Brad. Needless to say, I've heard quite a lot about you." She smiled, "All good."

He took her hand. "I can say the same about you. We obviously share a friendly acquaintance."

Meagan raised her hand. "I plead guilty. What more can I say about my favorite people?"

Cindy smiled happily. "I was in the area, so I thought I'd do a quick drop-by. And what a great day for a hike. Almost makes me wish I had the gear to do the same. Sandals wouldn't do, especially when I see what you're wearing. (she looked at Brad) And you're similarly dressed. You'd laugh at me on the trail."

Then, as quickly as she had arrived, Cindy gave Meagan and Brad each a hug and left, saying she had things to do. Thirty minutes later, Brad parked his car at the park, and they soon stood at the start of the trail. Just past the trailhead was Leisure Falls, the park's largest waterfall. During heavy spring rains and snow melt, it ran like a mini Niagara

Falls, throwing a cloud of mist and spray. On this late Fall day, it showed little spirit and quietly burbled over the large slab of rock beneath it. A second waterfall flowed just as quietly, with a pool of water bubbling below. After crossing a wooden bridge, they walked beside Roberts Creek and Clack Creek water courses, both with waterfalls, cascades and bridges crossing them. Further on, Brad pointed to a broad view of a stream and several pools below, all looking like a National Geographic scene, albeit without exotic wildlife. On a bench, they sat gazing at the creek as it flowed to the Salish Sea.

"This is so beautiful," Meagan murmured. "And so peaceful. All that can be heard are running water and bird sounds. It feels so good to be here together."

He reached for her hand and said, "It certainly does, sweetheart, and we'll do it often."

She nodded enthusiastically. "I *hope* so."

They gazed smilingly into each other's eyes and then happily, hand-in-hand, continued up the trail as if in their own secret garden.

They had walked only a short distance when they heard a dog yelping, followed by a loud shout. "*No.*" Rounding a turn in the trail, they saw a large dog lunging at a much smaller one. A young woman tried to hold the dog back by its leash. She screamed, *"No, No,"* as it snapped at a small Pomeranian being held on a leash by an elderly man. To escape the large dog, the smaller one had run behind the man's legs. As Brad watched, the man fell down, tripped by the leash. He quickly ran forward, shouting and loudly clapping his hands. He reached the dog in time to grab it by the collar and hold it away from the smaller one, now under the man's legs.

He held onto the struggling dog's collar as it lunged against his grip, trying to bite him. Not a nice dog. Then, looking at the woman, he said, "I'm going to hold onto your dog while we walk away."

Meagan bent to help the man as Brad held a palm toward the dog and sternly commanded, *"No"* before releasing its collar as the woman pulled back. “This dog shouldn’t be on these trails if it doesn’t behave better,” he said. “It’d be in your best interest to train it. Otherwise, you could face legal consequences, such as if that man had been badly injured.”

The woman nodded anxiously. “I’m very sorry this happened. It’s my sick friend’s dog. I agreed to take it for a walk. It’s the first time, and I won’t do it again.”

He walked back up the trail as Meagan helped the man to his feet. She had unwrapped the leash and lifted his dog from under his legs. Then, holding his arm, she helped him to stand and said, “Are you alright? You took a nasty fall.”

“I’m okay,” the man replied. “A close call, no damage done. (he pointed) I think I’d best be getting back to my car.”

They walked with him to the parking lot, he being a bit unsteady as he carried his quivering dog.

The man put the dog in his car, turned and said. “I can’t thank you two enough for your intervention. I’d hate to think of what might've happened if you hadn’t come along.”

“The woman said the dog belongs to a friend of hers,” Brad explained. “She did me a favor, taking it for a walk. She wasn’t aware of the dog’s disposition.”

The man looked intently at Brad. “I've seen you somewhere.” After a moment, put his hand on Brad’s arm. “The newspaper. I’ve seen your photo and read your column. I forgot your name.”

Brad held out his hand. “Brad Webster.”

The man smiled, shook his hand and said, “Gregory Hibbard. And rest assured, I’ll be reminded of your help whenever I read the paper.”

Brad took Meagan’s arm, “Your other helper is Meagan Atherton.”

Hibbard shook her hand. “You were a great

help. Thank you."

Then, without further adieu, he got into his car, waved goodbye and drove away. During their walk to his car, Mr. Hibbard said how he'd soon be leaving Sechelt and returning to England to pursue a family business endeavor with his brother. Brad's to-do list now included discovering more about this interesting man. Emma would know.

He turned to Meagan. "Are you up for going back and finishing the trail?"

"Yes, I want to see the rest of it. After that episode, the walk will do us good."

"Absolutely. By the way, did you notice the kind of car he drove?"

She nodded. "I think the big B indicated Bentley."

He nodded. "You're right, and you'd have to pay more than a quarter million dollars or more for a new one, which I think that one was."

After their hike, Brad drove to The Sunshine Coast Golf & Country Club, only a few hundred yards down the highway. Its sundeck, with umbrellaed tables and chairs, was a welcome retreat, especially during summer. At the service counter, he bought coffee and the last two muffins. As they took them to a table on the sundeck, he noticed two men sitting on a bench staring at Meagan. She seemed oblivious to their attention.

After pulling their chairs closer to the table and sitting down, he murmured, “You didn’t see the men sitting on the bench ogling you?”

“Oh, I saw them peripherally. I find it kind of humorous. But I often see ladies looking at you the same way. And you don’t seem to notice them either.”

“Well, there are definitely times when it is, as you say, humorous.”

She nodded. “When people are staring at me, I’m seeing the things they aren’t seeing.” (she pointed out) “Like those two eagles soaring above the tree line. At least it’s not us doing the staring. How *would* you feel if I stared at other men?”

“It’s an interesting topic. We’ve probably both been with people who did that. Maybe we’ve even been guilty of it ourselves, just a quick look, which is normal and okay. But it shouldn’t be a stare that’s rubbed in the other person’s face.”

She nodded knowingly. “An all too common relationship annoyance. And you’re right, a look is more respectful, but not a stare.”

He reached across the table and squeezed her hand. “Unless we’re staring at the same person for whatever.”

They both laughed, pleased at how the subject had produced a situation resolution without dutiful overtones. They then sat happily enjoying their coffee and muffins while taking in the natural surroundings. The near view took in a long course and a putting green; to the south was a wide view of the main course plus the Salish Sea and Georgia Straight beyond. The comfortable sundeck and its attractive, natural tableau encouraged returns, something they'd often do after hiking the park.

Later, at Brad's house, they were starving for each other and there was no stopping their passion. In the bedroom, they made love in a way that true lovers understand. As they lay blissfully in each other's arms, Brad kissed Meagan and said, "I know we've said it before, but it really is as if we've been like this together in another life. And I have a confession to make about my theory of living apart in our own homes. I've never loved someone as I love you. And I never thought I'd meet you. And now I can't imagine you not always being in my life. But everything is developing so fast we've never really discussed this part of it."

"I love you the same way, darling, and you've opened a subject we *should* be discussing. So let's talk some more after we shower." So saying, she took his hand and led the way to the bathroom for what she called a two-person splash and dash.

Later, as they sat comfortably in his leather recliners, she opened up, saying, “It’s wonderful to hear you say that you no longer feel that each of us living alone is the way for us to live and love. But the next step is something we have to be certain about. We’re both from breakups and not so long ago. Nevertheless, as far as my marriage is concerned I can honestly say I feel in every way completely freed from the entire episode. (she grasped his hand) “You’ve shown me a world of love and enlightenment, a world of our own, what I needed to be me again.”

He squeezed her hand. “We *are* on the same page, and as far as *my* current feelings about my breakup are concerned, I’m not——”

“Brad, can you honestly say you have no lingering doubts about your breakup?”

“Meagan, my relationship with Karen was

completely different than ours. We were both too engrossed in our work lives, and we developed different lifestyles, social priorities, separate lives and, as it turned out, separate goals. And I could never be absolutely sure about what she really wanted. That is until she flat out said she wanted to get married and start a family, knowing full well that I didn't want to go down the same path. We were so completely opposed in our expectations we were faced with the only choice we could make, and that ended it."

She nodded understandingly. "We're so fortunate to have met at this stage of our lives and can plan our future together. And to think it mightn't have happened if Alexis hadn't invited you to my place."

He raised her hand and kissed it. "When I told Alexis I'd help on painting day, the only thing on my mind was helping to get some work done. But after meeting you and spending time together in the kitchen getting to know you, I knew I wanted you in my life. As time passed, I even thought about it as a manifestation: think about it, believe it, and it will happen. My focus centered on you to such an extent that it soon clearly showed me what had been missing in my life. It was you. And the more time we spent together, the clearer it became. I could never love anyone as much as I love you."

"Brad, I feel it, too. Call it spiritual, but I know we're meant to spend our lives together."

They sat for a moment, happily gazing into each other's eyes. They both knew the next chapter of their lives wouldn't be carried out simply with talk. The flame would be carried in their hearts and souls, knowing they'd always be together.

Brad's tasteful pizza dinner was a slam dunk, so much like Meagan's that it couldn't be anything else. After dinner, they talked ardently about their future until almost midnight, when he drove her home. Arriving there, they undid their seat belts, leaned over and held each other. They couldn't yet call it a day. They talked about the day's outcome until Brad kissed her and, summing it up, said, "It's been a wonderful *life-changing day.*"

Chapter Twenty-Seven

On the following Saturday, Brad did what he had been wanting to do for weeks. He and Meagan had committed to each other, and there was no putting it off. That morning, he went to Wakefield Jewellers and purchased a stunning, one-carat diamond engagement ring. It showed excellent color and cut, was one of the nicest rings in the store, and one of the most expensive. Brad could afford the best for Meagan.

In the later part of the afternoon, he and Chris hiked Kinnikinnick Park and then went across the road to Blue Ocean Golf Club for a glass of beer on the patio.

After a quenching mouthful of beer, Chris said, "So, what's going on with you and Meagan? Both times I phoned you this week, she was at your place, or you were at hers. Was it a coincidence, or do you see each other every night?"

Brad chuckled. "We see each other two or three times during the week and most weekends. She spends time with her sister as well, and, zip, another week goes by."

"I know. I've had a crazy week thanks to a special rate I advertised in both papers. Then, there are the usual injuries that keep me busy. But you and Meagan are getting pretty involved in your relationship. Have you got any plans for the future?"

Brad put down his glass. "It's a coincidence that you should ask. I think I proposed to her last Sunday."

"You *think* you did? Either you did, or you didn't."

"I said I wanted her in my life, and now I'm going to prove it. This morning, I bought an engagement ring at Wakefield Jewellers, and I'm going to ask her to marry me."

Chris reached out his hand. "Well, congratulations, my friend. I was wondering if it'd happen."

"I've never before felt about any woman the ++way I feel about Meagan, and I'm doing something about it. I don't want to risk losing her." Chris nodded. "It sounds like you've discovered a soulmate." "That and more," Brad said with feeling.

"I thought my wife Carolyn and I had a good relationship," Chris said. "She was twenty-nine, and I was thirty-six, both old enough to know how things should be. But after eight years, we divorced last year. I think I've told you this before. My point is that to be a soulmate, you have to support her hopes and desires as much as your own. It's about choices, sometimes benefiting you, sometimes her. The choices you make in your relationship will determine your soulmate level. It's like being best friends and really loving, really caring."

Brad nodded his understanding. That's how *I* love Meagan, and *she* shows it in the way she loves *me*.

After another beer and discussing other relationship matters without getting too complicated, they finished their drinks and went their separate ways.

Meagan was having dinner out with Alexis; Brad had the evening to himself. He'd use the time to design a follow-up form that would be a handy adjunct to his day timer. He also had some follow-up paperwork to do for next week's business contacts.

At eleven-thirty-five, his phone rang. "Hi, Brad, Will here. Sorry to wake you."

"No problem. I haven't been to bed yet. What's happening?"

"I know who the midnight snooper is." He paused. "Go on," Brad said impatiently.

"I was walking back from the convenience store, and I saw something move beside Meagan's house, and it wasn't an animal. I went to the opposite side and poked my head around the corner and saw a guy standing there. I took out the flashlight I had in a side pocket of my cargo pants and shone it on him."

"*And* what did he do?"

"He said, 'Hi Will, how are ya?' His name is Art Herchmer. I met him a few times at the pub."

"This is important, Will. Was he doing anything or carrying anything? Or did he act aggressively at all?"

"No."

"And what did you say?"

"I asked him what he was doing there, and he said making sure Meagan was safe."

"Do you know anything about him?"

"Only that he lives in Davis Bay. In fact, he said he had to catch the midnight bus to Davis Bay."

"Did he leave then, while you were there … you saw him leave?"

"Yeah, he said, see ya."

"Thanks, Will. This is very helpful information. Someone will be in touch tomorrow."

Moments after Brad hung up, his phone rang.

"Brad, I just heard voices beside my house and I—"

"It's okay, Meagan. I was *just* about to call you. It was Will talking to a guy named Art Herchmer who was–"

"Oh my God! He's Adam's brother."

"Your ex-husband's brother?"

"*Yes*."

"According to Will, he only checked to make sure you were safe."

Meagan sighed heavily. "That doesn't make any sense. He hardly knows me aside from seeing me when I was with Adam."

"Another surprising thing is that Will knows him."

"This is too weird," she said breathlessly. "Art isn't a bad guy, just different. He's retarded, and worships his brother."

Brad had another thought. "You don't suppose he *could* be dangerous, do you?"

"No, he's shy and gentle and has level-two retardation that prevents him from doing many kinds of work. He lives with his parents in Davis Bay."

"Meagan, everything's going to be cleared up. I'll contact the RCMP tomorrow morning, and we'll get to the bottom of this. They'll want to talk to you. Will you be okay tonight?"

"I'll be fine once I get this straightened out in my mind. Darling, I wish you were here."

"I do, too, but things are going to be alright. You should be able to sleep better knowing the source of the sounds you've been hearing."

"He's harmless. I'll be fine."

"Then sleep well, sweetheart. I'll call you in the morning. I love you."

First thing Sunday morning, he phoned the

Sechelt RCMP office and talked to an officer about Art Herchmer and what Will had told him. The officer asked if Meagan would agree to talk to him. He said she would and gave the man her phone number.

Then Brad phoned Meagan. “Good morning, darling. I talked to an officer who would like to have a short appointment with you at the RCMP office or your place, wherever it’s convenient for you. I told him today would be an easier time to contact you, it being your day off work. So I suppose he could call anytime.”

“I hope he *does* call today. I’d be happy to see him anytime today before I go to your place so I can put this to rest, SAP.”

Brad was looking forward to serving Meagan a special Sunday dinner he had had in his mind for a couple of days: sockeye salmon with brown rice and a Caesar salad. Dessert would be pecan pie with or without whipped cream. He had also invited Alexis, but she demurred, saying she was tired and hadn’t slept well.

At five-thirty, Meagan arrived looking fresh and alluring as usual.

He looked at her appraisingly. “I must say, you look marvelous, my dear. A true chef d’oeuvre.”

She smiled. “Well, it sounds like something related to the kitchen.”

He laughed. “It’s a French word meaning masterpiece, and you are *my* masterpiece.”

She laughed and shook her head. They kissed tenderly before he led her to the living room, where the coffee table was set with glasses and a chilled bottle of white wine. When they were seated on the sofa, he turned to her. “So, did the police phone you?”

“The RCMP officer phoned me this morning, and I told him I’d be happy to have our appointment at my place in the afternoon if he had time. He said he'd come by at two o’clock. There was something impressive and sobering about seeing an RCMP officer in full uniform walk into my house."

"I'm all ears. Tell me everything."

She told how the officer took notes and wrote names and times. He asked if she wanted to press any charges. She wouldn't. Both Will and Art Herchmer will be interviewed, and if nothing more serious is found, Art will get a warning. If he does it again, he could be charged with harassment. When everything has been looked into, Meagan will be given the results.

"I just hope it will be the end of it," she said worriedly. "I don't want to hear any more nighttime sounds unless it's a friendly, foraging animal."

"I'm sure this *will* be the end of it," Brad said encouragingly. "We'll just have to wait and see what the police have to say."

She nodded, looked at his new shirt, and said, "I like your shirt's alternating white, black, and purple fine lines that give it a nouveau-pattern look, which no doubt it is, and wonderful chef attire."

Brad chuckled as he poured wine. "It's an Arnold Palmer, and the color is heliotrope purple, a color I've never heard of before. You, of course, know it's purple, but to me, it looked blue. You probably know that some men tend not to be as good as women at recognizing the nuances in certain colors."

"I have seen it. A man came into the store one day and looked around before picking out a woman's pink sweater. He brought it to the counter and said his wife likes red. But it wasn't red, more like a darkish pink. I told him so, but he bought it, saying his wife would love it."

Brad took a sip of wine and gazed at his glass for a moment.

She reached for his hand. "You seem a bit nervous tonight. Is everything alright?"

He hesitated and looked deeply into her eyes. "Meagan, I never thought I'd meet you, and now I can't imagine living without you. Your love has completely changed my previous way of thinking and brought me to this point."

She held his hand more firmly, seeing the emotion in his eyes.

He turned, reached behind a sofa pillow, withdrew a small box, opened it, and presented it to Meagan. "So, sweetheart, will you marry me? Can we plan our wedding?"

She took a moment to absorb the full impact of the sparkling diamond. "Brad, you wonderful man, *yes,* I'll marry you." She looked at the ring again and excitedly gushed, "*It's gorgeous.*"

He took her hand and slid the ring onto her finger. He lifted her to her feet, wrapped her in his arms, kissed her warmly, and said, "My dream came true."

"Mine, *too*, darling," she said, returning his kisses.

"I *was* going to ask you on your birthday, but I

didn't want to wait until then." He looked at the ring. "The jeweler said you could take it in for sizing or a new setting if you'd rather."

"I won't have to. It fits perfectly and looks wonderful."

Their engagement made for an extraordinarily upbeat evening. During dinner, they felt as if they were already married. The feeling later carried to the bedroom, where they excitedly expressed their love as never before. Then, in happiness and contentment, they talked until midnight about their engagement and who they'd tell. Alexis had that morning invited them to dinner at her place the following Saturday. They'd tell her then.

With the next day being a work day, Meagan hadn't planned on staying overnight. It hadn't been Brad's plan either, he being preternaturally on the ball weekday mornings, especially Mondays. Later, lying in their beds, they reveled in the excitement of their engagement and wedding plans.

Chapter Twenty-Eight

It'd be a busy week for the couple, fueled by the added inspiration of wedding plans. By the end of it, Brad had wrapped up a particularly full and newsy column. For Meagan, their engagement had given her a heightened level of enthusiasm, especially when customers pleasingly commented about her engagement ring. On Saturday, before going for dinner at Alexis', Brad bought two bottles of Appleton Rum and drove to Will's house. When he knocked on the door, Will opened it, looking surprised, "Well, look who's here."

Handing Will the bagged bottles, Brad said, "This is for helping to identify Art Herchmer. Meagan and I both appreciate it."

Will looked at the contents. "Whoa, nice, thanks a lot."

With that, Will stuck out his hand. Brad shook it and, with little more to say, he got into his car and left.

Later, while driving to Alexis' place, he told Meagan about it, and she agreed he'd done the right thing. "Did you tell him we're getting married?"

"No. He'll find out soon enough."

As they drove, she leaned over, put her hand on his knee, and said, "Before I forget, I want you to come to my place for dinner on Wednesday."

He smiled and pressed his hand on hers. "Thank you, my love. Any particular reason?"

"Not really. My turn, and I love having you with me at the table," she said.

"My feelings exactly, sweetheart. I'll be looking forward to it."

Alexis got her first glimpse of change when she opened her door. "Hi, you two. I'm so glad to see you." She paused, looking at them. "Well, come in, don't stand there grinning like a couple of Cheshire cats. What's going on?"

Meagan gave Alexis a hug. "We wanted to wait

until tonight to tell you."

She held out her left hand. "We're engaged."

Alexis stood with her hand to her face, looking from one to the other.

Stepping forward, she pulled them into her arms. "I can't tell you how happy I am that you've done exactly what I hoped you'd do. You two are *absolutely* meant for each other. Oh, I'm so glad. Let's have a drink."

As they sat enjoying white wine, she smiled excitedly. "So when's the wedding?"

"It won't be long now, but there's so much to plan," Meagan said.

"Now that you're engaged, will you begin living together?"

"We only today sorted out that stage of things." She looked at Brad.

"We haven't had a chance to plan very much yet," he said. "But Meagan will soon take up residence at my house. For the rest of the proceedings, maybe we need a planner."

Alexis put up her hand. "I'll be your planner. You each own a home, so decide which one you want to live in and sell the other one. As I see it, that's the biggest decision you have to make. You'll each own your own assets until such time as there is a normal progression toward a certain amount of it being held in common or whatever. It's called loving and sharing. How's that?"

Brad smiled. "You make it sound so easy, but it *is* a big decision. We've at least made some headway and will live together in my home that will become our home."

He reached over and squeezed Meagan's knee.

She nodded happily. "We haven't worked out the details of selling my place, such as the best time to begin."

Alexis said, “I hope you two aren’t going to have one of those engagements that go on for years.”

Meagan looked at Brad. “It won’t take long to figure out the when and how of things.”

Alexis clasped her hands together. “Oh, so much to look forward to. Let’s have dinner.”

On Monday morning, after the regular office meeting, Brad began leaving for an appointment when Emma intercepted him.

“Brad, have you got a moment? We haven’t talked for a while.”

“Sure, Emma, what’s up?”

“I don’t know your circumstances socially, but the Rotary Club is having a hospital fundraiser on Friday evening, and I thought I’d ask if you’d be my escort.”

She had gone from subtle flirtation to now testing his social potential.

“Well, Emma, my personal circumstances have changed. My girlfriend Meagan and I've become engaged.”

She put down her coffee cup. “Well, that*’s* a *big* change. Please accept my congratulations.”

“We plan on getting married quite soon. We haven’t decided on a firm date yet.”

She laughed. “Well, I guess that’s a definite *no* to my question.”

“You shouldn’t have any trouble getting an escort. In fact, I know a guy who’d be perfect for you. Do you by any chance know my friend Chris Hansen, the veterinarian?”

“Yes, I do. We carry his ads regularly, and I've spoken with him many times. A nice guy.”

Brad tilted his head. “So would you consider him? He’s single and unattached, and I know he likes you. He once said I was lucky to have you as editor.”

She sat back in her chair. “I didn’t know he was

single or anything else about his private life."

"I'm sure he'd be happy to escort you. Should I ask him?"

"If you think he'd be interested, ask him to phone me, and we can discuss it."

He left the office with a grin on his face, feeling a bit like a matchmaker. *They'd make a great couple,* he thought. Chris said he wasn't busy on Friday evening and would be happy to call her.

Shortly after Brad got home from work, Meagan called, anxious to tell him details in the police report she received that day.

"Art admitted to being at the house several times and once peaked through the store window. He was also the one who phoned the store. And get this, he doesn't know why he did it. He also let the air out of your tire. Again, he doesn't know why. I think there might've been a confused jealousy issue involved. Apparently, when I moved to Sechelt, Adam told him to keep an eye on me and let him know how I was doing and, maybe, *what* I was doing. Anyhow, Art decided to cover both bases. It became a favorite pastime for him in his confused world.

"So what will the police do?"

"Art has been warned that another instance of his surveillance could result in me pressing charges. And that's the complicated part. There are peace bonds, restraining orders, and stay-away orders. I'd need a lawyer, and I don't want to go there. The police believe this is simply a nuisance situation, something that can be handled with a warning. I feel the same way about it."

"And what if he does it again?"

"Art's a harmless soul. He once said he had a crush on me and would take me away from Adam, and Adam was standing there when he said it. He said it was funny. I don't fear him at all. I think we should leave it as is."

Both of them were relieved by the outcome, and when they finally said goodnight, they looked forward to being together for dinner on Wednesday.

That evening, Brad sat in a recliner, thinking about the outcome of recent events. *None of it involved Mason*, he thought, *but when might it? I'd like to find out for certain where he is, and I know Jeffery will be happy to help me do it. I won't be satisfied until I know where he is.*

As he drove to Meagan's house Wednesday evening, he felt they should take the short road to their wedding. They were happiest with time spent together, each of them inspiring the other in planning their marriage, as well as how and when they'd begin living together.

As they stood together in Meagan's kitchen, Brad broached the subject of her upcoming birthday and his plans for a birthday dinner at his place.

"Sweetheart, your birthday's a little more than a week away, and with our engagement being front and center, we haven't discussed it much. I'm planning a birthday get-together and invited Alexis and the Megalos. It'll be the perfect time to tell Eric and Connie of our engagement."

She threw her arms around him. "Thank you, darling. You realize it's going to be my big four-zero. I've never really thought about being in my forties. It sounds so much older than the thirties."

"Meagan, you look like a low number in the thirties, so I wouldn't give it another thought."

"I could say the same about you. You're much younger looking than your age. We're both fortunate."

He grinned, "Good genes, good luck."

For dinner that night, Meagan had prepared lamb stew, something Brad particularly enjoyed. After dinner, they sat having tea while more carefully discussing marriage details. She'd move in with him before listing her house. It'd give him time to do fix-ups, such as replacing the vinyl tile in her kitchen. She'd do some touch-ups. Brad had a sip of tea and put down his cup. “Meagan, with so many last-minute details, I don’t want things to be in a rush for your sake.”

“My sake? Why?”

“Because of your house, efficiently selling it, and so on.”

“I can’t *wait* to sell it. Besides, I’ll be living with you at your place.”

He nodded. “*Our* place. Maybe we should elope, simply get married. We could do it tomorrow.”

She giggled. “Tomorrow? We’d have a hard time doing that in Sechelt on the weekend. Vancouver, maybe.”

“We could go to Vancouver tomorrow, get a nice hotel room, and be married on Friday.”

She shook her head. “It isn’t that easy. We’d have to get a license and then track down someone to marry us. It'd be hectic and unmemorable, and we wouldn't have our friends and family with us, so I vote no deal."

He smiled happily. "You're right, my darling. We'll have a wedding that will be memorable."

Being the practical couple they were, the evening ended with an increasingly smoothened road to their future, further manifesting the shape of things to come.

Chapter Twenty-Nine

Sunday dawned cold and overcast, a typical November day with an inch of snow on the ground, a terrific day for hiking. But Brad had better things to do. He'd be preparing Meagan's birthday dinner and setting up for his special guests. The Megalos had recently returned from their Greek holiday and were looking forward to being at Brad's, especially with it being Meagan's birthday. Alexis had been looking forward to it all week.

Meagan had slept over and enjoyed one of Brad's sumptuous ham-and-egg breakfasts. She'd return later with her evening clothes to help out.

He had everything ready for the big night: food, drinks, and especially Meagan's birthday gift that he set on the hall table. At Wakefield's Jewellery, he had purchased a two-strand pearl necklace and wrapped the jewellery box in sparkling silver and gold lamé paper that bespoke of it being something special for someone special.

After breakfast, he sat in a recliner, enjoying coffee as he did a rehash of how he wanted things to go that evening. Everything seemed to be perfect. As he was finishing his coffee, his friend Jeffery called. “Sorry to call you on a Sunday, but I've got some news. One of the radio networks has an item you should know about. Our friend Mason is no longer.”

Brad was confused. “What do you mean no longer?”

“Apparently, Mason was driving his car like a madman last night on Highway 3 between Princeton and Keremeos … probably drunk but didn't survive. No complete news yet. I just now got this from a reporter who heard it. A truck driver told police that Mason was trying to get around his eighteen-wheeler on a curve and ran head-on into another big rig. Both truck drivers are okay. Manson wasn’t so lucky and has been keeping me up to date. Quite an ending, eh? It should be in the papers tomorrow.”

“It’s going to take a while for this to sink in,”

Brad said. “I thought ex-cons had a set period of having to be in place or at least get permission from their parole officer to leave town. To ignore parole and then drive like a maniac does sound like Mason, alright.”

“It sure as hell does. But it at least takes him out of the equation.”

“Jeffery, thank you very much for calling. This will remove Mason from my mind starting right now. Thanks again.”

A madman like Mason now being dead didn’t seem a possibility. But according to Jeffery’s informant, it *had* happened. Brad would no longer feel Mason’s threat lurking, as if on the other side of dark glass. He'd think no more about it, and, as important, he'd tell no one, not even Meagan, at least not yet. He thought *it'd be better to forget about Mason entirely.*

In the afternoon, shortly after two o’clock, Meagan returned with her evening clothes and a small overnight case. She looked radiant, wearing tan slacks and a brown, long-sleeve blouse, what she called her work clothes. Brad took her things, placed them carefully on the sofa, and held her in his arms. "You look so gorgeous. I want to hold you and not let go."

"Thank you, sweetheart, but we wouldn't get much done," she said, kissing him. "What can I do to help?"

"Not much, actually, at least not right now. I've moved the furniture back a bit for circle dancing. We have a little more than two hours to get ourselves ready. "

She raised an eyebrow. "Circle dancing?"

"Yes, you know, Greek circle dancing. You've seen it where people dance arm-in-arm, like in the movie Zorba the Greek. I have the music, and Eric will show us how to do it."

She smiled and happily said, "It'll be fun to have

a new dance experience together."

In the kitchen, he showed her the skewers of lamb for souvlaki. A large pot of water sat on the stovetop, awaiting the usual brown rice. A Greek salad with generous amounts of feta cheese was already in the fridge, including a cherry cheesecake for dessert.

She looked appraisingly. "You've been busy. I'll set the table and then help you in the kitchen when you need it."

After a light dusting and setting the table, she said, "Brad, I'm going to change and get ready. Then I'll come back and cheer you on." So saying, she hurried upstairs.

It soon became time for him to change for dinner. She had dressed and was busy in the bathroom doing final touch-ups. As he put on his shoes, he heard her leave the bathroom and go downstairs. After some perfunctory attention to details, he, too, descended, anticipating a joyful evening.

He looked radiantly dressed with a pale blue, shaped-fit Bugatchi dress shirt and tan slacks. As he came down the stairs, Meagan looked up at him and smiled lovingly. She, too, looked outstanding in a beautifully patterned shift dress, emphasizing her statuesque beauty. He stepped down, reached out, and held her close.

"You look wonderful," he said. "My beautiful birthday girl."

"Thank you, darling. You look wonderful, too."

As they strolled to the kitchen, the doorbell rang. Alexis arrived looking happy and excited; her attractive lilac-colored jacket and dress reflected her usual flair. In one hand, she held a brightly-colored flower arrangement. In her other hand, she held a small, attractively-wrapped birthday gift.

"Sorry to be early," she said. "But time dragged on, and I didn't think you'd mind."

Meagan kissed her on both cheeks. "Alexis,

you're a mind reader. After I set the table, I could see something was missing: *flowers*, and minutes later, you arrived with them." She put water in a vase, placed the flowers in it, put the arrangement on a ceramic coaster in the center of the table, and stood appraising them.

"They look perfect. Thank you, sis."

"They do look nice. And you're very welcome."

She then held out her birthday gift. Meagan thanked her and looked at the gaily wrapped package. "It looks enticing," she said as she placed it on the hall table.

"I hope you'll like it."

"I don't think there'll be any doubt about it," Meagan said. "I'll open it when we're all together."

In the kitchen, Brad poured wine. Alexis followed him and watched. "And what are you going to have," she enquired.

"I bought some ouzo that I'll have with Eric.

You'll enjoy Eric and Connie. They've become great friends."

Alexis took glasses of wine for herself and Meagan into the front room as Brad straightened the pot of water on the burner.

Moments later, the doorbell rang. Brad opened the door with a flourish. "Yasou, come in, my friends," he said as he shook Eric's hand and hugged Connie. "I'm so glad I can finally welcome you to my home."

As he took their coats and hung them in the hall closet, Meagan embraced each of them. Connie wished a happy birthday to Meagan and handed her a package, while Eric passed a bottle of ouzo to Brad.

"Thank you both," Meagan said, placing the package on the hall table beside others.

Brad gestured. "I'd like you to meet Meagan's sister, Alexis. "These are our friends, Eric and Connie Megalos."

Then, leading Alexis and the Megalos" into the living room, he made them comfortable on the sofa, each with a glass of wine. In the kitchen, Brad poured ouzo from his bottle for Eric and himself – his watered down as usual. Eric said nothing about his own ouzo not being used. It'd be Brad's treat.

When all were seated in the living room, Brad squeezed Meagan's hand and looked at her as if to suggest they should go with the flow for a while.

Connie's eyes, however, caught sight of her ring.

"That's a beautiful ring. Have you some news to tell us?"

Brad spoke up. "We were going to surprise you tonight and tell you that we're engaged. And I know you'll be pleased to know our marriage won't be put off until who knows when."

Eric raised his glass. "That's the *best* news in a long while."

Alexis nodded happily. “It’s what I've been hoping for ever since I saw the two of them together. They were meant to be together. I have never seen a couple more suited to each other. Even so, if Meagan hadn’t grabbed Brad, he’d be in my sights even though it wouldn’t do any good. (she laughed) I’m not Meagan. But we’ll be like brother and sister when the marriage takes place, a beautiful extended family.” She raised her glass.

Eric downed his ouzo.

Brad took Eric’s glass to the kitchen, and because he politely didn’t remonstrate about wanting his own ouzo, Brad again poured his. When he returned to the living room, Alexis, Connie, and Eric were still admiring the ring. Brad gazed at it once more, pleased that it was indeed an attractive, one-carat diamond ring and the quality he wanted for Meagan.

He went to the hall table, picked up the gifts, and placed them on the coffee table. “I think it's a good time for the birthday girl to open her gifts."

Meagan enthusiastically looked at them and reached for the one that had been the first one there. "I know this one's from my honey." When she opened it and saw the elegant pearl necklace, she gasped,

"Oh my gosh, what beautiful pearls." She looked at Brad with amazement. "Thank you, my darling. I'll look forward to an occasion to wear them … starting with tonight." She held the necklace to her neck. "Will you do it for me?" She then quickly dashed to the bathroom mirror. Returning to the living room, she did a slow spin to show the necklace.

"You could get a job at a fashion magazine showing off things like that," Eric said. Everyone nodded.

Meagan happily regarded the other two gifts. After saying, "eeny, meeny, miny, moe," she began unwrapping the Megalos' gift, which was a light-blue, hand-knit cardigan.

She held it in front of her. “It’s beautiful and just what I need in this colder weather. It’s very thoughtful of you. I know there’s a lot of work in this.”

“It took me forever,” Eric chuckled, adding, “You know who made it.”

Meagan happily looked at Connie. “Thank you, thank you both.”

As she began to open Alexis’ tastefully wrapped gift, she saw Alexis’ excitement.

“I’m trying to imagine what this could be,” she said as she began to open the box.

“Any guesses?” Alexis teased.

“No, but I’m sure I’ll be surprised.”

When a jeweler’s box came out of the wrap, she looked at Alexis. “I hope you haven’t gone overboard on this, sis.”

Alexis smiled. “Open the box.”

She slowly opened the lid and saw the gift, so

relevant – a set of pearl drop earrings matching the necklace.

As she lifted one of them and held it in front of her, she turned to Alexis.

“Not only am I surprised, I’m blown away by these incredible matching earrings. I’m tempted to say you shouldn’t have, but I’m so glad you did. I’m sure it isn’t an amazing coincidence.”

“Brad told me he bought a pearl necklace for your birthday. So I thought pearl earrings would be a perfect compliment to them. They’re matched pearls from the same jeweler.”

“Thank you so much, Alexis. I love them,” she said, removing her earrings and replacing them with pearls. “How do they look with the necklace?”

The consensus was that, especially on her, the pearls made a statement of elegance and style.

“Thank you all again,” she said glowingly. “These are such lovely gifts.”

While the conversation continued, Brad went to the kitchen and checked the rice he had earlier added to the boiling water. Then, going further into his chef mode, he went to the fridge, got the skewers of lamb, and placed them on a metal tray. On the patio, he heated and cleaned the grills before placing the skewers on them. He once said he feels something primal in cooking meat – smelling it and hearing it sizzle.

Eric suddenly appeared."I wasn't sure if you were cooking already. That's a nice barbecue. Reminds me to get a new one."

Brad gazed at his truncated finger. "I can't get over how good the finger looks, not like an obvious accident victim."

"It's stiff, but I can use it by moving that part of the palm," Eric said as wiggled it more like a peg than a finger. "I can't complain, and I'm hardly aware of it."

Then he broached the ever-lingering question, "So when's the big day? Soon, I hope … while we're still young." He laughed, adding, "I hope it will be in

Sechelt so we can attend."

Brad nodded enthusiastically, "It *will* be in Sechelt, and we haven't yet set a date. It won't be long."

When the meat had cooked, he and Eric walked into the house.

"Honey, you're just in time," Meagan advised. "The rice is done, and I've put it in a bowl."

He put the skewers on a serving tray and said, "Everyone, have a seat, and we'll serve dinner. Meagan and I'll sit closest to the kitchen."

She placed the bowl of rice on the table while he brought the lamb skewers and salad. She then filled everyone's wine glass before sitting down. Lifting his glass, Brad said, "A toast to friends and happiness at the table." This was quickly seconded by Eric's "Yia Mas *good health*." Brad suggested they help themselves and pass to the left to prevent a traffic jam, which brought out a snicker from Eric.

"You sure you weren't a traffic cop at one time? It *is* a good way to prevent a traffic jam."

Brad said, "*You'll* have to prevent a traffic jam tonight when you show us how to Greek dance. I did it once in Greece, and I want us to do it tonight as a dance of celebration. We can dance to music from Zorba the Greek."

"Connie and I used to Greek dance all the time with a couple of friends here who have since passed on," Eric said. "When we were in Greece this last trip, we danced the Syrtos, considered to be the national dance of Greece. We'll do it tonight. It'll be fun."

As dinner progressed, talk revolved around Greece – both Alexis and Brad had been there – and the experiences were enjoyable. Eric and Connie gave a rundown about their trip that Eric said would be their last.

After dinner, everyone relaxed in the living room with coffee or tea while Eric explained some of the fundamentals of dancing in Greek style.

Chapter Thirty

The enthusiasm shown for the couple's engagement was understandable. It wasn't often that the guests had the opportunity to attend an engagement celebration for two people who were older, yet younger, two dynamic and attractive people whom they held in high esteem.

Connie spoke up advisedly. "I think when you decide to get married, it should happen sooner than later and not wait until who knows when. A timely marriage shows the strength and sincerity of a couple's feelings. Eric and I met in July and were married in September. We knew we always wanted to be together as husband and wife."

Eric nodded enthusiastically. "I'd have married her the same week I met her."

Connie shook her head. "No, you wouldn't have, and neither would I. We had things to work out just like Meagan and Brad do."

"I'd like them to be husband and wife before I leave for Mexico," Alexis intoned. "They've loved each other long enough to know when to take the next step."

Meagan raised her hand. "We're only newly engaged, and, as Connie said, there are many things to consider and work out. We really can't set a date yet." She looked at Brad. "But we're getting close."

He nodded, "The biggest thing we have to think about is the sale of Meagan's house. Something to consider is that a furnished home always shows better to potential buyers. She has some nice furnishings that will attractively set the place off. So they'll remain there, and Meagan will begin living with me."

"We'll put it up for sale and see what happens," she said.

Brad stood up and said, "So now, for the next part of the evening's program, Eric will show us how to dance Greek style." He walked to the stereo and put on music from Zorba the Greek.

Eric organized everyone into a dance line with forearms on each other's shoulders, and he began showing them how to dance the Sirtaki. He slowly had them do the steps in unison. Then he had them do two more attempts, which proved to be too great a challenge for the evening's uninitiated. He next introduced the Zorba, another popular Greek dance. The ensuing general confusion ended up with them simply doing steps together, barely in time with the music and with a couple of near stumbles, but no casualties.

"Whew, I need to sit down," Alexis said. "That's more exercise than I've had in quite a while. Those leg movements forward, backward, sideways, and then speeded up, whew!"

She was quickly joined by Connie. "I can usually do both dances."

Eric used the moment to make a suggestion before the dance mood evaporated. "I think the engaged couple should do an engagement dance for us."

"Alright," Brad said enthusiastically. "We'll do it to Zorba the Greek."

Meagan looked at him happily. "And hope Zorba approves."

He put the music on, and they quickly went from what looked like a slow two-step to what resembled a speedy polka, enthralling everyone with the smoothness of their moves as they glided across the floor. They were in supreme harmony, and their dance ended to happy applause.

"That was truly *dynamic*," said Connie. "But how about something *slower?*"

Meagan smiled at Brad. "Remember that piece you played when you said it described us? Let's dance to that."

Brad put the music on, and, while looking into each other's eyes, they glided across the floor. It became apparent to everyone that they were seeing a true dance of love.

Alexis put her hand to her face as tears welled. "They're dancing to a song that sounds like them."

"What song is it?" Connie said.

"I'm sure you'll remember it … the Seekers, *I'll never find another you.*"

When their dance ended, Alexis went to them and wrapped them in her arms, wiping her tears.

Connie, too, had teared up.

Eric sat transfixed. "Those two are meant to be together if anybody is." And then, looking at Connie. "We danced like that before *our* wedding day, too, didn't we?"

"And we've been dancing ever since," she said while gesturing. "I know you two will be doing it as well."

Brad nodded. "No doubt about that."

Meagan put an arm around his waist. “We’re both dancers and always will be, even if the day comes when we have to help each other do it.”

They all laughed when Brad said. “We’ll call it the cane dance.”

The evening ended with the couple’s rapport spawning feelings of comfort and happiness in their guests. Their loving togetherness promised the kind of marriage and partnership that would be comforting for family and friends alike.

When the guests had left and a modicum of cleanup had been done, Brad and Meagan sat on the sofa, relaxing and discussing their future.

She turned to him. “I really want to know if you think we should put my house up for sale first or get married first. I can see it being less complicated if the paperwork has my name on it during the selling period instead of perhaps having to change it down the road.”

She leaned her head on his shoulder. "We're a couple, and I don't want it to sound like anything else. I'll sell it as Meagan Webster. I like the sound of it."

He nodded in thought, "It sounds wonderful."

She reached for his hand. "So it means we get married first and sell it later."

"I think it'd be the best way of doing it. At this time of year, and until springtime, real estate is customarily slow, and it could take a few months. I agree with Connie. We know we want to get married, so let's not put it off." "But when?" said Meagan.

"What could be better than doing it in early December before some people go away on vacation? We'll invite all of our family and friends. (Brad's daughter) Marie can stay here, and the rest of us live here in town."

Meagan cuddled up to him. "We've got *some* family and our friends. It'll be celebratory and convivial, and I can't wait."

As is so often the case when many hours are spent organizing and setting up for a big day, it quickly arrives. The wedding took place on Sunday, December 9, at Brad's house, where Reverend Ian Rogers pronounced them Mr. and Mrs Webster. Invited guests included Alexis, Marie, Eric and Connie, Meagan's friend Cindy, and Chris and Emma. Brad's friend Jeffery said he wished he could attend, but he was already socially committed.

At the reception, Brad told about Mr. Hibbard's dog being attacked at Cliff Gilker Park and how he and Meagan had interceded.

"And last week," he said, holding up an envelope, "I received this from him."

Holding a sheet of paper, he read, *"Dear Brad and Meagan. I'll always be grateful for your help at Cliff Gilker Park. It's a rare thing to have it so quickly, given that so much is needed. The other reason I am writing is to tell you I am moving to England to assist my brother in his business startup.*

My Sechelt home has been sold, and I am flying to London next week.

Enclosed is a $10,000 bank draft that is a wedding gift of appreciation and a wish that you both will find the happiness you so richly deserve.

Yours sincerely,

Gregory Hibbard

PS – I've enclosed my contact information and invited you to call me if you are ever in London."

"So who is he?" Chris said.

"All I know about him is what I heard from Emma." Brad looked at her. "Do you remember me telling you about the incident with his dog on the trail?"

Emma nodded. "As I said at the time, he's a wealthy developer who retired to Sechelt five years ago with his wife. Unfortunately, she died a few months ago."

"He was a real gentleman," Brad said.

Two days after the reception, the newlyweds flew on a Harbour Air float plane to Vancouver for a three-day mini honeymoon at the popular L'Hermitage Hotel, known for its service and amenities. They went to their favorite restaurants, did a walk around Stanley Park twice, and at The Queen Elizabeth Theatre saw a performance of Giselle, a ballet in which Meagan had once performed in the corps de ballet. The performance and her memories of it had, in some scenes, almost brought her to tears of fond remembrance.

For their final evening, Marie joined them at Five Sails Restaurant. The fine dining and harbor-side location had always made it one of Brad's favorites. The menu had something for everyone. Its delicious entrees and water-side views made it a special evening for the extended family.

“If we all lived in Vancouver, we could, of course, do this more often,” Brad said, smiling.

“But you're the one who moved, Dad,” Marie

said, looking at Brad.

He nodded. "A case of now not being in the habit, I'm afraid."

The evening ended with them all agreeing that what was necessary was to get into the habit of visiting each other's homes. Brad hoped it'd happen – t*ime will tell.*

Before Christmas, Alexis had excitedly invited Brad and Meagan for Christmas dinner. The day turned out to be sunny, almost warm, and they all went for a walk in Kinnikinnik Park. Meagan had suggested it'd be a perfect thing to do on such a pleasant Christmas Day. And she was right.

Arriving back at her condo, Alexis enthused, "A walk like that is a great way to work up an appetite. Now there's lots of time before dinner. I've got some mixed nuts with mostly cashews that go great with wine or beer." She looked at Meagan and Brad.

They had had a late brunch and declined.

Meagan had a glass of wine and Brad a beer. They were both somewhat absorbed, wondering what Alexis had planned for dinner. They could tell by the floating aroma that Alexis had obviously had a busy morning, maybe even outdone herself. Now, with dinnertime approaching, she chatted from the kitchen.

"I'm glad I got an early start on dinner prep," she said cheerily. "These sorts of things can often take more time than expected. But I'm well ahead of it today."

She could never be called a whiz in the kitchen. Her meals were the kind that could be called regular fare or same-old. She satisfied herself with whatever served its purpose while at the same time making up some remarkable combinations. But today, she'd make a real Christmas Dinner.

She walked into the kitchen and lifted the lid on the Crock Pot. "David and I (referring to her late husband) used the Crock Pot only occasionally. It's the first time I've used it since coming to Sechelt. Being in the storage locker pretty much kept it out of my mind. I'm glad to be able to use it for dinner today."

She picked up a large spoon, gave the ingredients a stir, placed the lid on the kitchen counter, and said, "Okay, you two, have a seat. Dinner's ready." Then, using oven mitts, she carefully carried the pot to the dining room and placed it on a mat in the center of the table.

"Whew, that should do it," she said. Then, stepping back and looking at her guests, said, "Now, I want you to enjoy my cacciatore. The recipe called for chicken, but it being Christmas, I thought turkey would be more traditional. I had some help from Independent's meat department in getting some turkey breast."

She stepped back triumphantly and poured three glasses of wine before sitting down. To the surprise of both Meagan and Brad, the meal turned out to be a winner. A delicious potpourri of turkey breast and vegetables. The dessert was delicious, too. Alexis served pecan pie, saying, “You may not know this, but pecan pie is a traditional Christmas dessert.” Neither Brad nor Meagan had heard of the tradition.

Later, while having tea, Meagan said, “I can’t get over how nicely cooked the breasts were.”

Alexis cocked her head. “I checked online and found they can be cooked separately and then put in the pot with the vegetables for a while before serving. Who would know?”

“Well, dinner was wonderful,” Meagan said, with Brad nodding in agreement.

As the evening progressed, the trio discussed, among other things, the sale of Meagan’s house and their upcoming honeymoon to Mexico. On the subject of their honeymoon in Mexico, Alexis also had some news. She had for some time been preparing for her move there whether her house was completed or not.

"I've discovered a moving company that more or less routinely ships furniture for Canadians retiring to Mexico. As you know, my home is being built at Lake Chapala, and I've found a mover that goes there often. Chapala is a very popular place."

Brad nodded. "I read in a travel article that out of the ten top places to live and retire in Mexico, Lake Chapala is number one. It has the most developed expat English infrastructure in Mexico. It has amazing group activities, top-notch medical care, and is close to Guadalajara if and when you need it."

Alexis smiled. "So it's no surprise that I'd want to live there. And here's the big news: "I've been given a couple of available dates for the move, and Meagan, you told me the date you're going there for your honeymoon, and I booked a shipping date that will put me there in time to enjoy some of it with you."

Meagan and Brad raised their hands in happy unison.

"That's great news," Meagan said. "We'll be

able to discover new adventures together."

Alexis had been anticipating her move to Mexico to the extent that she had been spending more time than usual practicing Spanish. And that night, she showed an enhanced facility for it at the door, hugging Meagan and Brad and saying, "Buenas noches, te amo." (Good night, I love you.)

By the second week of January, Brad and Meagan had been living together as husband and wife for a month. They kept busy, finding time to sell some of Meagan's smaller items as well as replace the vinyl tile on her kitchen floor. There remained one more item to address – the faded bedroom ceiling. The painter would be Brad. Yet the month wasn't entirely about repairs and adjustments. It included acknowledgment of Brad's milestone fiftieth birthday on the twenty-third.

"Don't invite everyone," Brad explained to Meagan. "I don't think at my age it's fair to expect people to come bearing gifts."

"But it's an important birthday," she said. "Part of your scheduling for retirement. Like a job monitor recording date and time. I'll only invite Alexis."

Having determined the scope of the celebration, Meagan made it a special celebration for three. Dinner was beef stew, one of Brad's favorites, with wine sauce broth. The trimmings included potatoes, carrots, onions, mushrooms, and bacon, all accompanied by sauvignon blanc wine. Dessert was another pleaser, with – what else? – chocolate cheesecake. The look on Brad's face confirmed his inimitable pleasure. He reached for her hand and said, "Meagan, my darling, thank you for the best birthday dinner ever."

After dinner, they discussed Alexis' upcoming move to Mexico. She had been in a flurry of activity for the past couple of weeks. The mover's truck would be taking the larger items in two weeks; the smaller things and collectibles would go with her in her SUV.

“In the meantime, I’m happy to help her,” Meagan said. “I wish she wouldn't stress herself so much. But she did a good job of searching for the best options in shipping companies.”

“What did she decide to use?”

“After looking at the benefits of shipping by land, sea, or air, she chose land for its good selection of routes and truckers. She even considered following the truck but realized it was a no-go.”

Brad nodded. “Good thing.”

In mid-February, the couple went on a ten-day Mexican honeymoon. Before leaving, Brad completed a comprehensive and ambitious backlog of material for his next two columns. He also contacted realtor Fred Vallevand to have Meagan’s house listed for sale at the beginning of March.

The couple spent eight days visiting the Lake Chapala area. Alexis had moved to Mexico in early February when her home there was only half finished. She had been invited to stay with her new friend Marcia until completion. They had met while Alexis shopped for property to build on.

Brad and Meagan enjoyed a comfortable room in a nearby motel. Most of their time was spent with Alexis exploring local sites and checking the progress on her not-yet-completed house. Near the end of their stay, they rented a car and slipped away for a two-day visit to Guadalajara. Alexis had been there before and suggested that while there, they should also go to Tlaquepaque.

“You’ll love it there,” she said. “It’s less than 10 km southeast of Guadalajara and features a historical outdoor market with art galleries, craft shops, and delicious dining experiences. It’s all set among cobblestone paths and decorative arches. It’s an experience not to be missed.”

The couple went to the city and the market, spending a truly adventurous two days. Meagan especially liked some of the Mexican wraps she saw.

"So colorful and beautifully woven."

On their last day, they were again in Guadalajara for their flight home, driven there by Marcia and accompanied by Alexis. The sisters had a tearful parting, with promises to each visit the other, and Alexis happily made Brad party to it. Later that day, they arrived in Sechelt on a connecting Harbour Air float plane from Vancouver. Brad felt a bit nervous about something he had arranged with Chris and a Sechelt printer. Would it be there? As the couple got off the plane, Meagan said, "It feels so good to be back – the air, the water, the overall feel. I'm excited about being home again."

Brad used his phone to call a cab, and they were soon pulling into their driveway. "Back to our home sweet home," Brad enthused.

They paid the driver, thanked him, and carried their luggage to the house, where Meagan stopped with her hand to her face. She shook her head slowly as she read a banner hanging over the door:

"Dearest Meagan, welcome back to our house that you've made into a home."

She turned and looked at him with amazement. "I'm at a loss about what to say."

"I had Chris do it."

"But, Brad, it *was* a lovely home *before I* moved in."

"And you've made it a more comfortable home," he said, setting the last piece of luggage in the door. "It needed *you*."

She thought for a moment. "I think what you're saying is that it simply needs the *two* of us. The comfort of our combined love."

He kissed her warmly and said, "You're absolutely right, my darling." He then swooped her up in his arms and stepped into their world meant to be.

THE END